CW01643452

Embroidery
48 new designs

Marshall Cavendish

CONTENTS

Published by Marshall Cavendish Books Limited
58 Old Compton Street
London W1V 5PA

© Marshall Cavendish Limited 1972, 1973, 1974, 1975, 1976, 1977, 1978, 1979, 1980, 1981, 1982, 1983, 1984, 1985

Printed and bound by Grafiche Editoriali Padane S.p.A., Cremona, Italy

ISBN 0 86307 317 4

Patterns There are three types of pattern for you to work from: trace patterns, graphs and charts. Explanatory notes and diagrams showing how to use each of these methods, together with instructions for making up the projects, can be found on pages 54-57.
Materials Now a word about material requirements. Anchor Stranded Cotton. **1**.044 (2) Carmine Rose. The first number (in this case, **1**) always refers to the area on the pattern where the yarn is to be used. This is followed by the manufacturers' colour number (044). The next figure in brackets refers to the probable number of skeins or balls of yarn you will need, followed by the colour description (Carmine Rose). So, for the example given, you will need 2 skeins of Anchor Stranded Cotton, colour number 044, for area number **1** of the chart, trace pattern or graph. It's as simple as that.
Colours Certain designs are given with precise colour references — as, for example with the shading of leaves and flowers, where the relationship between tones is important. With other designs, however, colour is entirely a matter of personal preference. But do remember to be generous with the amount of yarn you use! Embroidery should always be rich and colourful.
Stitches The illustrated Stitch Library on page 58 should be extremely useful for new embroiderers, both to practise from and as a constant source of reference. In many of the designs, you'll find we suggest that stitches are worked in a free and impressionistic manner, rather than being restricted to a set shape. And you'll soon notice that embroidery stitches can be made to work for you creatively — just as paint can work creatively for the artist. Flat stitches catch the light. So, by changing the type of stitch you use and the direction in which you work it, you can easily alter colour tone and give your work extra perspective. You'll enjoy watching your embroidery come alive in this way!

Editor Liz Goodman
Art Editor Amelia Edwards
Embroidery consultant Margaret Beautement

Cover photograph by Steve Bicknell
Other photographs by: Atlantic Press Nos 28-30
Beta Pictures Nos 23, 38, 39, 40, 41, 42-45, 46
Camera Press Nos 1, 2, 3, 4, 5-10, 11, 12, 13, 14, 15, 16, 17-20, 21-22, 24, 25, 26, 27, 31, 32, 33, 34-37, 47, 48

Illustrations by Janine Kirwan

1

An elegant rose spray worked in cross stitch

Finished Measurement: The rose spray measures about 5″ x 9″.
Fabric: White evenweave linen, 20 threads to the inch. Measure the tray and allow 3″ on each measurement for turnings.
Threads: 1 skein of each colour. Anchor Stranded Cotton. **1.** 073 Light old rose; **2.** 074 Old rose; **3.** 07 Geranium; **4.** 066 Pale raspberry; **5.** 063 Mid-magenta; **6.** 085 Light cyclamen; **7.** 0295 Buttercup yellow; **8.** 0304 Gorse yellow; **9.** 0265 Moss green; **10.** 0258 Parrot green.
Needles: Tapestry no. 22.
Stitch: Cross.

An elegant rose spray has many uses. Simple to work, it is delightful placed to one side of a tray cloth, colourful mounted into a simple narrow frame or used as a repeating pattern on a cushion.

Oversew the edges of the fabric. Mark the centres of the area where the rose will be worked. For the tray cloth, mark a 5″ x 9″ area for the left side placing of the rose. Use three strands of thread in the needle. Begin working the flower head at the centre line. Each square represents one stitch. Each stitch is taken over two threads of the fabric in each direction.
When the embroidery is complete, press and make up with a plain hem as shown on page 56.

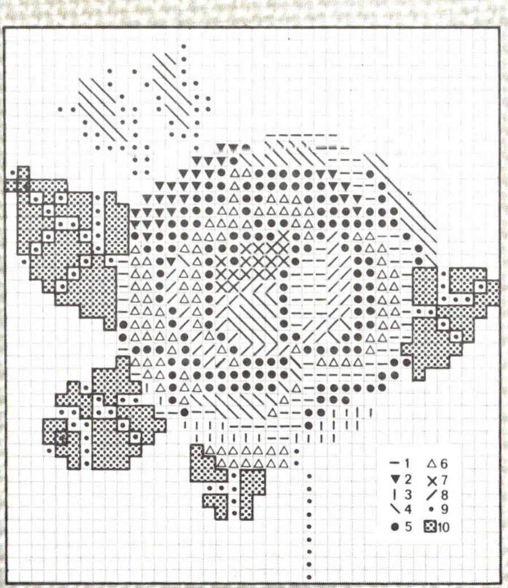

2

Trefoil design to repeat as a border, or work as a single motif

3

Graceful poppy spray, worked on a crisp white linen ground

4

Delicate hop trefoil embroidered on a plain traycloth

2

Trefoil design

Finished Measurement: 14″ x 18″.
Fabric: White linen, 16″ x 20″.
Threads: 1 skein of each colour. Anchor Stranded Cotton. **1.** 0245 Deep grass green; **2.** 0239 Deep Spring green; **3.** 0242 Mid grass green; **4.** 062 Mid magenta; **5.** 0100 Deep violet; **8.** 042 Mid Carmine rose; D.M.C. Stranded Cotton. **6.** 554 Light violet; **7.** 3685 Burgundy red.
Needles: Crewel no. 6
Stitches: Satin and stem.
A ring frame.

Two trefoil sprays repeat to make a border for a tray cloth. Separate them and use as spot patterns on a large cloth or singly as a pocket decoration.

Oversew the edges of the linen to prevent fraying. Run a tacking line to indicate the fold-line of the hem. Transfer the trace pattern to the linen as shown on page 54. Position the trefoil border two inches in from the left-hand hem line and about one and a half inches from the top and bottom. Work the embroidery with three strands in the needle. Where a figure 9. is shown use two strands of colour 5. and one of 4., threaded into the needle together. Work the satin stitch in the direction indicated in the trace pattern. Vary the slant of the stitch in the small sections of the clover head. The tension of the thread is very slightly loose, particularly in the long stitches for the leaves. This will prevent the ground fabric from puckering. On the leaves with contrast bands of colour, work the long stitches first. Work the narrow bands slightly into the already laid stitches. Press and make up as shown on page 56.

3

Graceful poppy spray

Finished Measurement: About 13″ x 18″.
Fabric: White linen 20″ x 15″.
Threads: One skein of each. Anchor Stranded Cotton. **2.** 0315 Tangerine; **3.** 0332 Light flame; **4.** 0335 Dark flame; **5.** 0255 Parrot green; **6.** 0254 Light parrot green; **7.** 0280 Muscat green; **8.** 0281 Dark muscat green; D.M.C. Stranded Cotton. **1.** 920 Red brown; **9.** 437 Ochre; **10.** 829 Dark olive green.
Needles: Crewel no. 6.
Stitches: Back, long and short, French knots, satin, stem.
A ring frame.

A graceful poppy spray is in colourful contrast to the white linen ground of a plain hemmed traycloth.

Oversew the edges of the linen to prevent fraying during working. Tack a line to indicate the hem of the traycloth. Draw the trace pattern onto tissue paper. Pin the design at the right of the traycloth about 3″ in from the tacked hem-line. The top of the flower head will be about 2″ from the top hem-line. Transfer the design to the fabric as shown on page 54. Use three strands of cotton throughout. Embroider the stems, leaves and seed-heads in satin stitch. Follow the direction of stitch indicated on the trace pattern. With colour 9 work in back stitch down the centres of the leaves. Outline the seed-head with stem stitch and colour 10. The flower head is worked in long and short stitch. Begin at the outer centre point of each petal and shape the stitches inward toward the centre. The fold-over of the petals is worked in satin stitch and satin stitch is used in colour 7. for the flower centre. With stem-stitch outline the centre with colour 9. and the edges of the petals with colour 1. Finish by stitching French knots over the embroidery. Press and make up as shown on page 56.

4

Hop trefoil design

Finished Measurement: 12″ x 16″.
Fabric: White linen 15″ x 19″.
Threads: 1 skein of each colour. Anchor Stranded Cotton. **1.** 0369 Cinnamon; **2.** 0386 Cream; **3.** 0378 Beige; **4.** 0255 Parrot green; **5.** 0351 Chestnut; **6.** 090 Petunia; **7.** 048 Pale rose pink; **8.** 0280 Muscat green; **9.** 0281 Dark muscat green; **10.** 0288 Canary yellow; **11.** 0402 White.
Needles: Crewel no. 6.
Stitches: Stem, satin.
A ring frame.

Oversew the edges of the fabric to prevent fraying. About 1½″ in from the edge run a tacking line to mark the hem-line. Tranfer the flower spray to the fabric as shown on page 54. Position the spray about two inches in from the right hand hem-line and one inch down from the top. Work with strands of thread in the needle. The flowers and leaves are in satin stitch, the stalks in stem stitch. Work the groups of calyx in very small satin stitches, first padding slightly. Press and make up with a plain hem as shown on page 56.

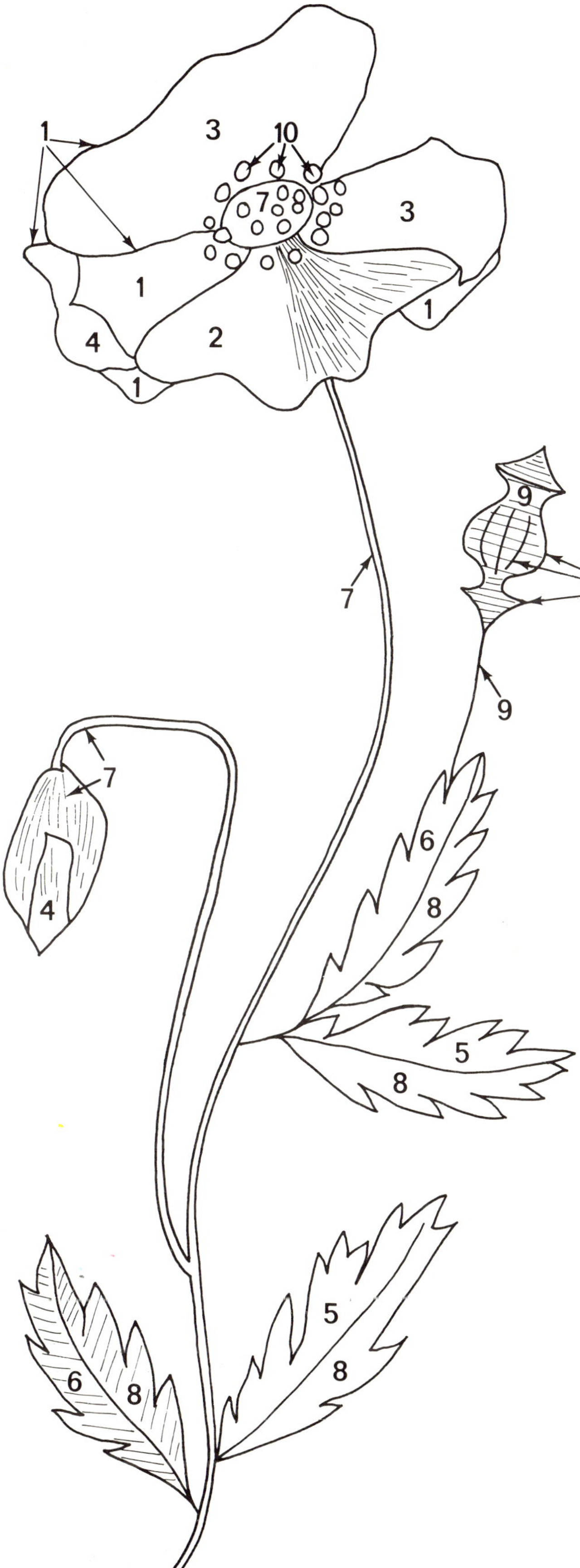

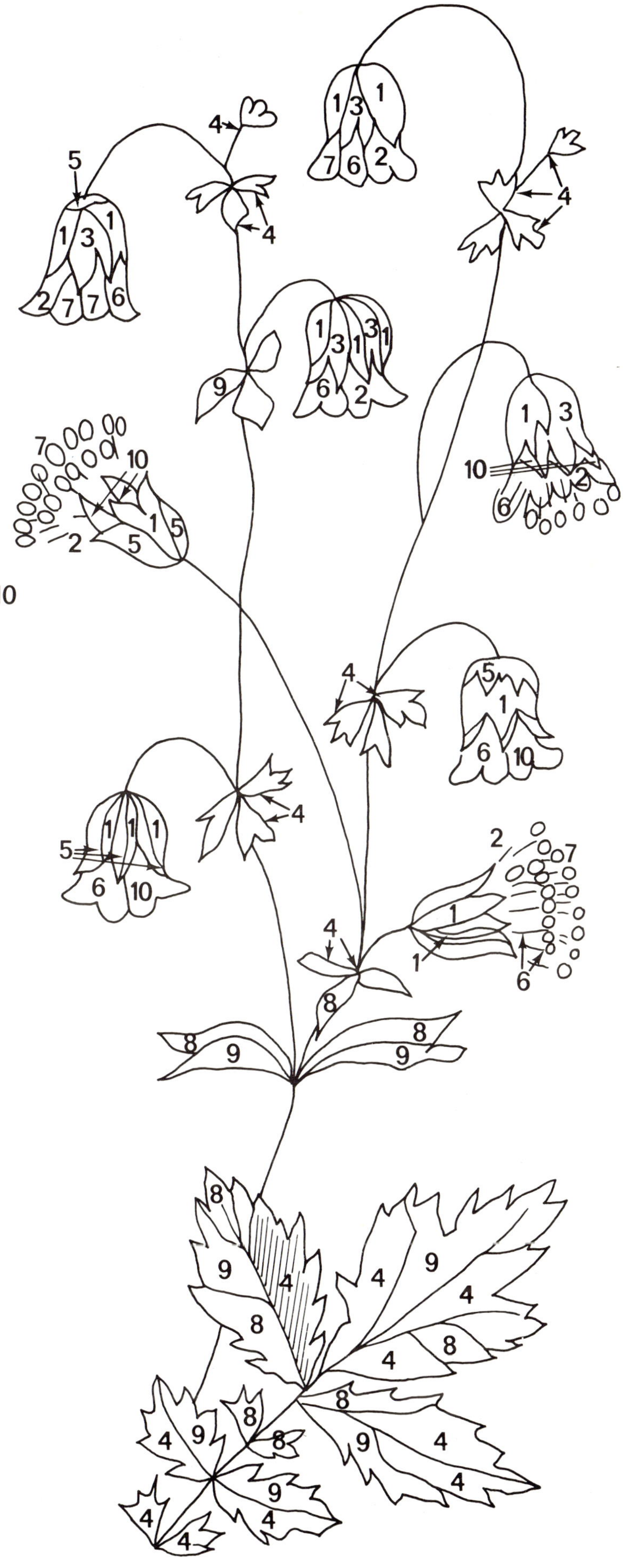

5-10

Six fruit and flower designs

Finished Measurement: About 7½″ diameter.
Fabric: Evenweave linen, 34 threads to the inch. 25½″ x 17″.
Threads: 1 skein of each colour. Anchor Stranded cotton. **Mat 1. 5.** 0298 Dark buttercup yellow; **10.** 0266 Light moss green; **13.** 0212 Dark laurel green; **17.** 0121 Delphinium; **19.** 0119 Dark periwinkle; **26.** Mix one strand of 2.(074) and 3.(076). **Mat 2. 1.** 0402 White; **5.** 0298 Dark buttercup yellow; **6.** 0350 Chestnut; **9.** 0269 Dark moss green; **11.** 0267 Mid moss green; **14.** 047 Turkey red; **21.** Mix 4(0300) and 14. **Mat 3. 4.** 0300 Gorse yellow; **6.** 0350 Chestnut; **9.** 0269 Dark moss green; **11.** 0267 Mid moss green; **12.** 0243 Grass green; **14.** 047 Turkey red; **20.** Mix 4 and 5(0298); **21.** Mix 4 and 14; **24.** Mix 1 (0402) and 2 (094). **Mat 4. 3.** 076 Old rose; **11.** 0267 Mid moss green; **13.** 0212 Dark laurel green; **16.** 0125 Indigo; **22.** Mix 18(0122) and 17(0121); **23.** Mix 16 and 17. **Mat 5. 3.** 076 Old rose; **7.** 0278 Light muscat green; **9.** 0269 Dark moss green; **10.** 0266 Light moss green. **Mat 6. 9.** 0269 Dark moss green; **12.** 0243 Grass green; **13.** 0212 Dark laurel green; **14.** 047 Turkey red; **15.** 044 Carmine rose; **24.** Mix 1(0402) and 2(074); **25.** Mix 14 and 15.
Needles: Tapestry no. 22.
Stitches: Cross and stem.

Six mats in very fine cross stitch. The fruits and flowers are sprays from the garland on the circular cloth (no. 47).
Oversew the edges of the fabric and work all six mats before cutting out. Run tacking lines to divide the linen into 8½″ squares. Again with running stitch, mark the centres of each of the squares. Work outward from the centre of the chart, so that the design is centrally placed on the mat. Each square on the chart represents one cross stitch. The stitches are taken over two threads of the fabric in each direction. Use two strands in the needle. Work stem stitch for the curving line on the blueberry design. Press and make up as on page 56. Decorate the hemmed edge with a row of stem stitch.

5
10
13
17
19
26

1
5
6
9
11
14
21
24

4
6
9
11
12
14
21
20

3
11
13
16
22
23

3
7
9
10

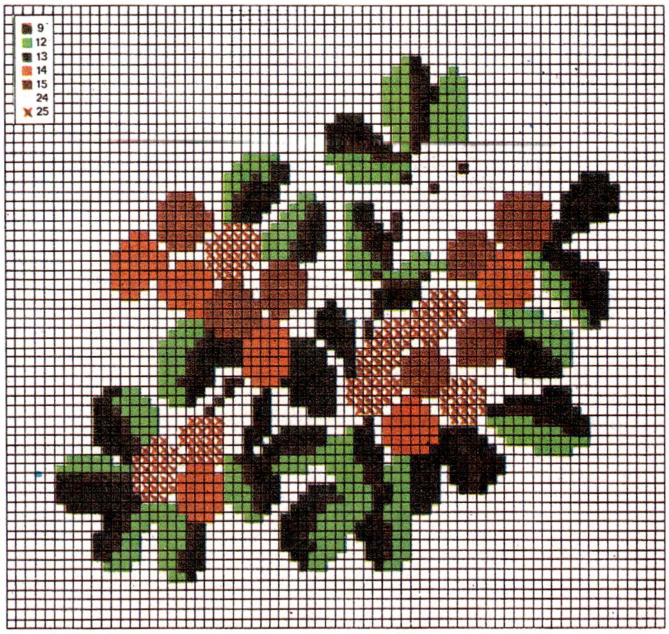
9
12
13
14
15
24
25

12

A striking design, quickly worked in woollen yarn, made up as a cushion or poncho

Finished Measurement: Design about 24 inches square.
Fabric: Poncho—fabric amount as shown on commercial pattern to fit your size. Floor cushion—White dress weight wool or linen, two squares of about 27″.
Thread: D.M.C. Tapestry wool. The number of skeins required is given in brackets after the colour number. **1.** 7257(3) Mulberry; **2.** 7139(2) Dark red; **3.** 7137(1) Light red; **4.** 7135(3) Salmon red; **5.** 7155(2) Cyclamen; **6.** 7367(2) Olive green; **7.** 7344(2) Bright green; **8.** 7484(2) Yellow.
Needles: Chenille no. 18.
Stitches: Detached chain, French knots, long and short stitch, stem.

Quickly worked and bold in effect, this striking design is stitched in a woollen yarn on white fabric. Work it as a floor cushion or buy a poncho pattern and embroider the front section before making up.

Transfer the design to the fabric, using the tissue paper method. The embroidery is worked with a single length of thread in the needle, except for the large, detached chain stitches. They are worked with one and a half threads. The four-ply wool splits easily into two two-ply strands. On the largest flower, colours 2 and 4, pack the French knots—colour 7—tightly at the centre. They are scattered lightly in the remaining three flowers. Care is needed in the working of the large detached chain stitches. Lay the work flat on a table so that the stitch is not pulled tightly and the ground fabric pulled out of shape. Press the embroidery as shown on page 55. Make up the poncho as shown on the bought pattern. Make up the cushion as on page 57.

11

Fine cross stitch roses, worked in rich colours, can be framed to add a touch of colour to a quiet corner

Finished Measurement: 7″ x 5″ inside frame.
Fabric: Hardanger cotton, 18 pairs of threads to the inch, 8″ x 10″.
Threads: 1 skein of each colour. D.M.C. Stranded Cotton. **1.** 320 Green; **2.** 890 Dark green; **3.** 945 Pale peach; **4.** 3688 Rose red; **5.** 321 Red; **6.** 3685 Dark rose red.
Needles: Tapestry no. 22.
Stitch: Long cross.
A ring frame (optional).
Picture frame. Inside frame 5″ x 7″.
Card for mounting.

A small, framed embroidery adds a touch of colour to a quiet corner. Long cross stitch makes for an unusual effect in the richly coloured flower spray.

Oversew the edges of the fabric to prevent fraying. Run a tacking line to mark the horizontal and vertical centres. Mark the five inch by seven inch area of the picture. Use four strands of thread in the needle. Begin the cross stitches one and a quarter inches from the top. Count outward from the centre line. Begin the pattern at the top and work down, using several needles threaded with the colours required in each row. Note that this is a long cross stitch, worked over two threads widthways and one lengthways. Press and make up as shown on page 56.

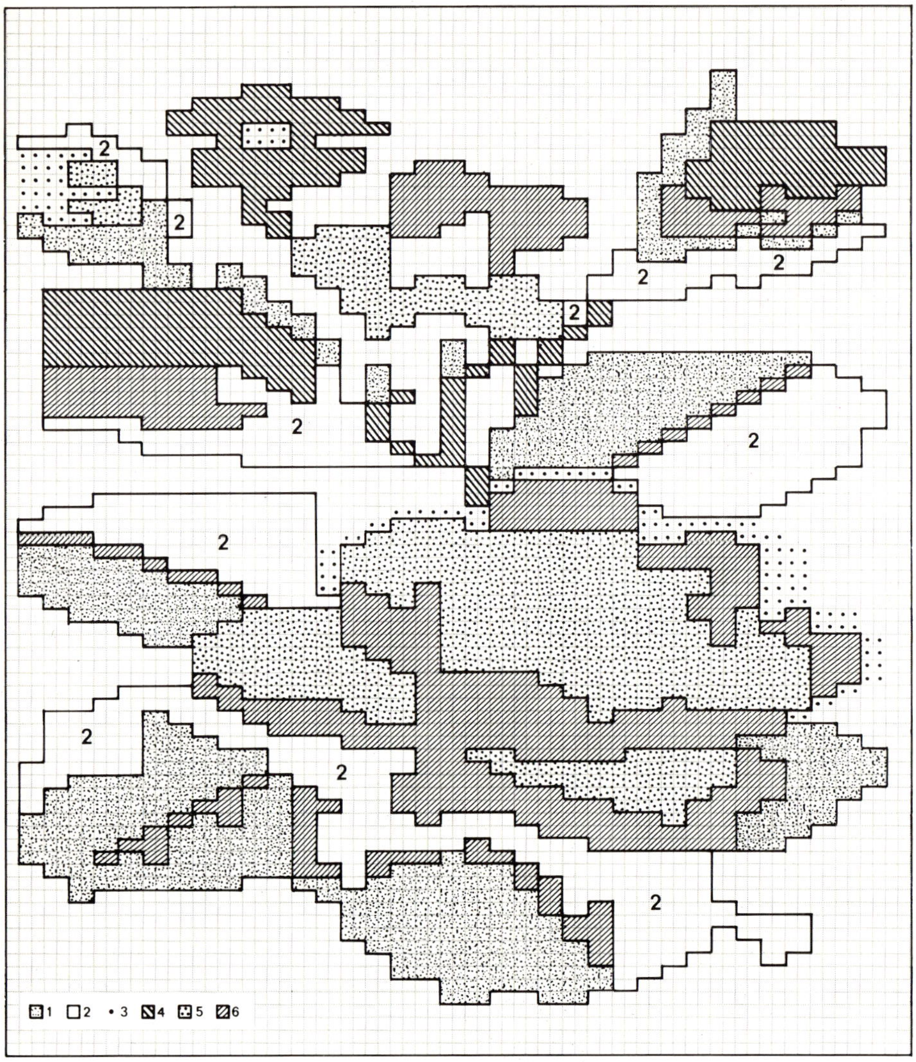

11 12

Fine cross-stitch roses, framed to add a touch of color to a quiet corner

A striking design worked in woolen yarn for a pillow or poncho

EACH SQUARE = 2″

13

Richly flowered drop-in stool cover in bold cross stitch

(chart below)

Finished Measurement: 16″ x $11\frac{1}{2}$″. Top of stool about 15″ x $10\frac{1}{2}$″.
Fabric: Single canvas, 10 threads to the inch. 20″ x 16″.
Threads: The number of skeins needed is in brackets after the colour number. D.M.C. Tapestry wool. **1.** 7727(2) Yellow; **2.** 7439 (1) Burnt orange; **3.** 7137(8) Cerise red; **4.** 7153(3) Cyclamen; **5.** 7353(3) Yellow/olive; **6.** 7351(4) Dull yellow/olive; **7.** 7359 (2) Dark yellow/olive. **Background** (13) White.
Needle: Tapestry no. 18.
Stitch: Cross.

A drop-in stool top has a side drop of about one inch. The unshaded flowers are quickly worked in bold cross stitch.

Oversew the edges of the fabric and mark the centres. Draw the outline for the chair seat as shown on the chart. The indented corners are not embroidered. Each cross stitch is taken over two threads of the canvas in each direction. Work from the top of the design downward. At the start of the pattern, work from the centre line outward. The following rows can be worked straight across from left to right or right to left, whichever is the easier. Cross the stitches in the same direction throughout.
Work back stitches to outline petals and flowers as shown on the chart. Stretch and make up as on page 57.

14

A cushion worked in surface stitchery, to match the stool

Finished Measurement: 17″ x 12″.
Fabric: Two pieces of ivory linen, 20″ x 15″.
Threads: The number of skeins needed is in brackets after the colour number. D.M.C. Stranded Cotton. **1.** 347(3) Red; **2.** 3688(3) Rose red; **3.** 900(1) Orange; **4.** 833(2) Light olive brown; **5.** 831(2) Olive brown; **6.** 829(1) Dark olive brown; **7.** 726(1) Yellow.
Needle: Crewel no. 6.
Stitches: Long and short, stem, chain.
Embroidery frame.

Make a cushion or picture in surface stitches to match the cross stitch footstool. Long and short stitch, stem and chain combine to fill the large flowers and leaves.

Mark the centres of the fabric. Transfer the design to the fabric, matching centres. The instructions are on page 54. Mount in a slate frame or oversew the edges of the fabric and mount in a ring frame. Three strands of embroidery cotton are used throughout. The three large flowers are worked in long and short stitch. Stitch toward the centres and space the stitches slightly. Outline the petals in stem stitch and colour 4. Fill the centre circles with colour 7, and outline with chain stitch and colour 6. The leaves are worked in the same way as the flowers and in the colours indicated. Stitch diagonally toward the centre vein. The small flowers are worked in surface satin stitch toward the flower centres. Outline with chain stitches—self colour for the rose coloured flowers and in colour 6. for the olive brown flowers. Press and make up as shown on page 57.

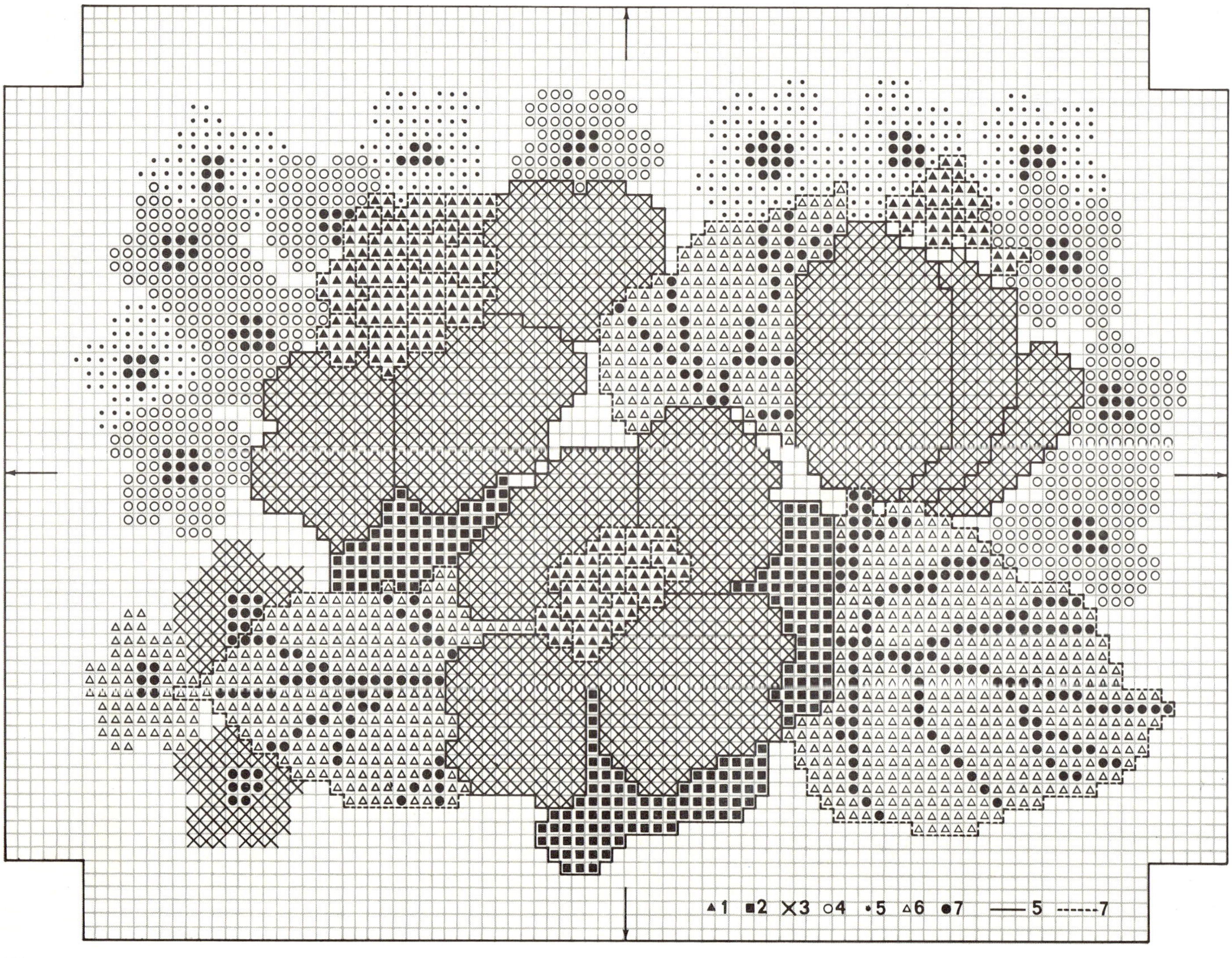

14

Cushion worked in surface stitchery

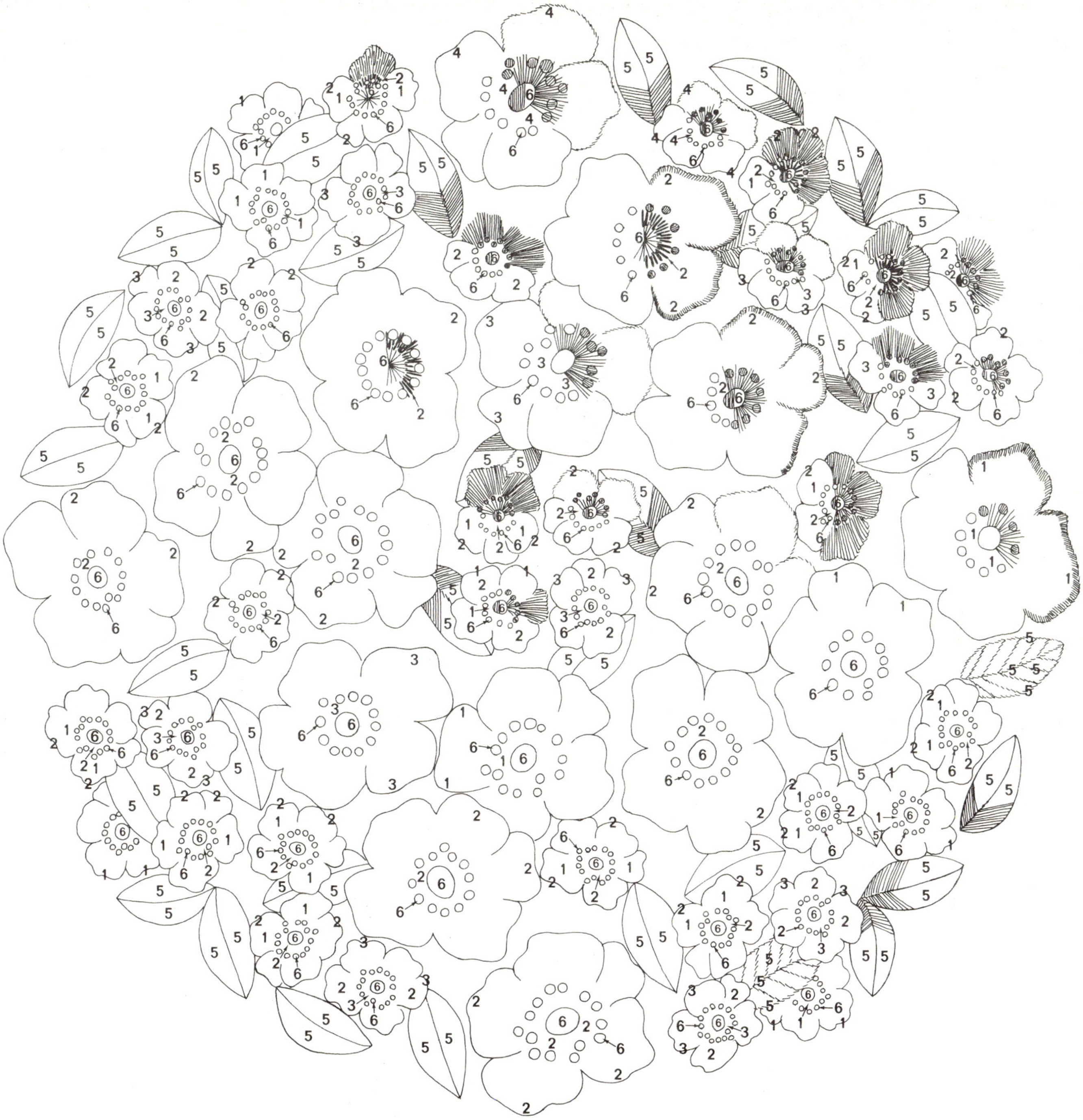

15

Blue flowered tablecloth

Finished Measurement: About 48″ square. Diameter of design, about 30″.
Fabric: White linen 52″ square. Turquoise linen for the eight applied flowers, about 20″ x 10″. Lightweight iron-on Vilene, 20″ x 10″.
Threads: The number of skeins is given in brackets after the colour number. Anchor Stranded Cotton. **1.** 0156(7) Azure; **2.** 0157(7) Dark azure; **3.** 0155(1) Mid azure; **4.** 0154(1) Light azure; **5.** 0258(6) Parrot green; **6.** 0304(2) Gorse yellow.
Needle: Crewel no. 7.
Stitches: Long and short, satin, stem. A ring frame.

An unusual tablecloth design with turquoise, blue and green in striking contrast to the white ground. The turquoise linen is quick to apply and sets off the sheen of the stranded cotton.

Oversew the edges of the white and turquoise fabric pieces. Mark the centres of the fabric. Transfer the design as shown on page 54. Appliqué turquoise flowers. On a separate sheet of tissue paper, trace off the flowers to be applied. Draw them close together in two rows of four. Transfer them to the turquoise fabric. With two strands in the needle work the embroidery as shown on the trace pattern. Press the embroidery face down onto a thick pad. Iron the Vilene to the back of the linen and cut round the outline of each flower. To apply the flowers: lay the cloth flat on a table and pin the flowers to the tacked outline. Put the cloth into the ring frame and buttonhole stitch by hand, or apply with a machine zig-zag stitch. The remaining flowers: embroider the small flowers in long and short stitch as indicated. Work from the high-point of each petal as shown in the Stitch Library, turning each stitch at an angle toward the centre of the flower. Fill the centres with satin stitch and work the stamens in satin stitch over the completed embroidery. Work the flowers with stem stitch outlines and outline the filled flowers with contrast colour stem stitch as indicated. Fill the leaves with satin stitch and work a stem stitch vein down the centre.
Press the cloth as shown on page 55 and make up with a plain hem.

15

Blue flowered tablecloth

Make two tracings of the chart and then fit the two pieces together as shown (right) to form the circular design

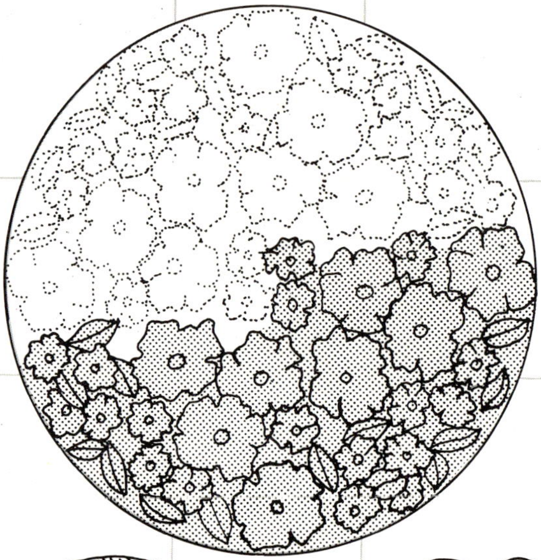

EACH SQUARE = 2″

16

Gay cushions - try the square design as a wall panel

Finished Measurement: Panel and square cushion about 18″ square. Round cushion about 10″ diameter.
Fabric: Double canvas 4 to 5 holes to the inch. 22″ square for the cushion and panel. Lining—21″ square. 14″ square of canvas for the round cushion. Lining 13″ square.
Thread: D.M.C. Laine à Broder. Number of skeins required shown in brackets after the colour numbers. **Square cushion and panel: 1.** 7317(6) Blue; **2.**(3) White; **3.** 7437(2) Orange; **4.** 7436(2) Pale orange; **5.** 7346(1) Green; **6.** 7344 Light green. **Round cushion. 1.** 7317(1); **2.**(2) White; **3.** 7437(1); **4.** 7436(1); **5.** 7346(1); **6.** 7344 (1).
Needles: Rug or heavy embroidery.
Stitch: Cross.

A gay panel of summer flowers to contrast with cool furnishings. Make it also as a square cushion with a matching round cushion.

For the square cushion or panel. Mark the centres of the canvas and the approximate area of the embroidery. Each square on the chart represents one stitch. Work from the top of the chart. Work across each row and on the pattern rows thread the needles with the colours required and work straight across. The pattern will build up as each row is worked. Stretch and make up as shown on page 57.

The round cushion. After marking the vertical and horizontal centres, draw a ten inch diameter circle. Work the cross stitch over the line rather than within it. Work across the rows as in the square cushion. Make up as shown on page 57. Part stitches will be taken into the seam when machining the circle. A length of thread close-couched round the edge of the cushion gives a corded finish.

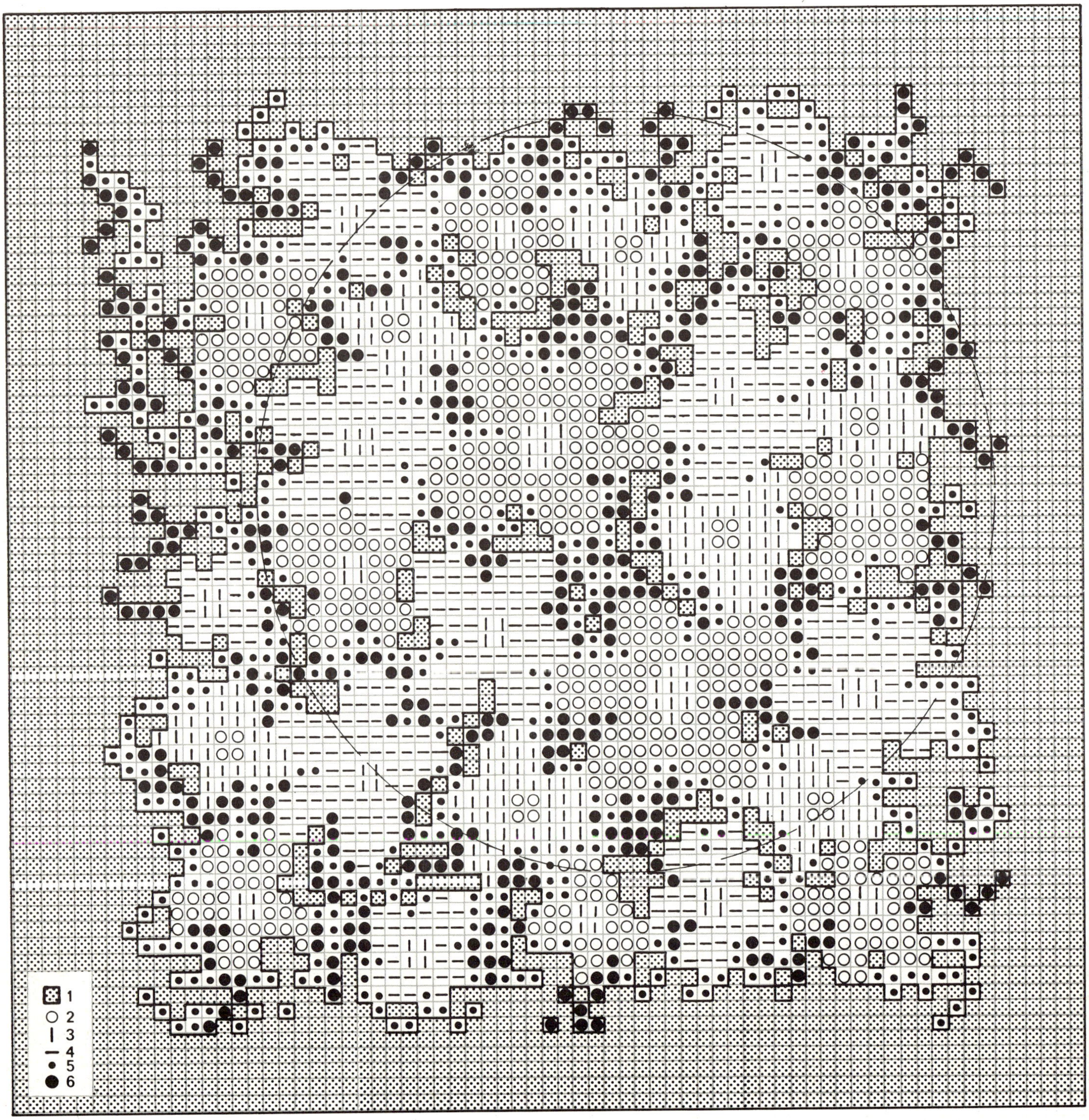

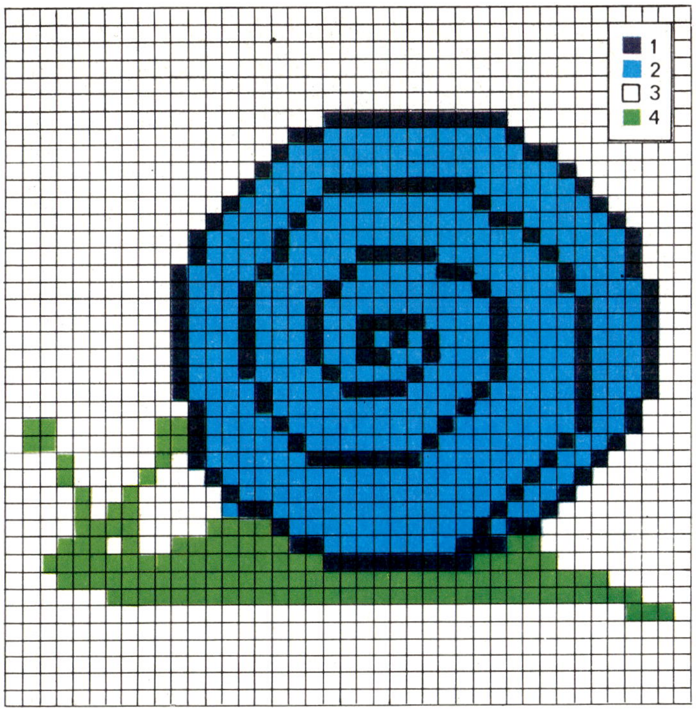

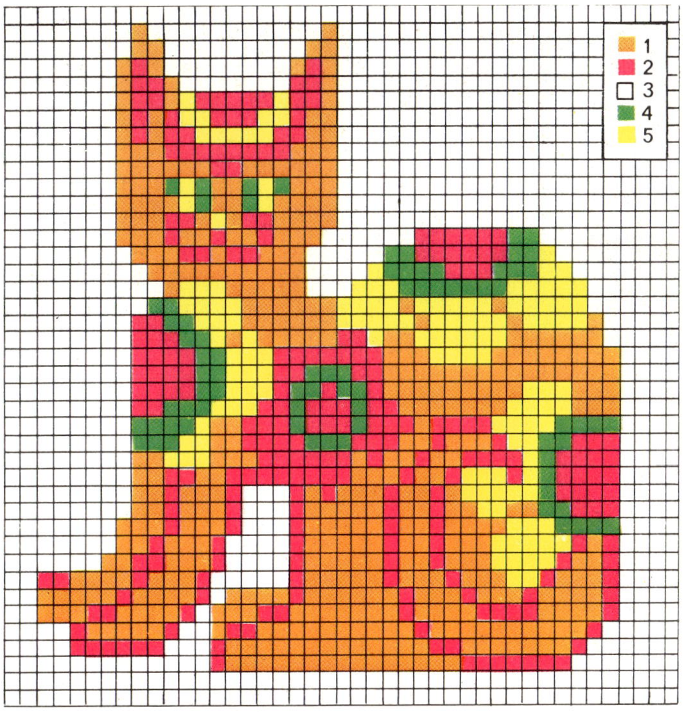

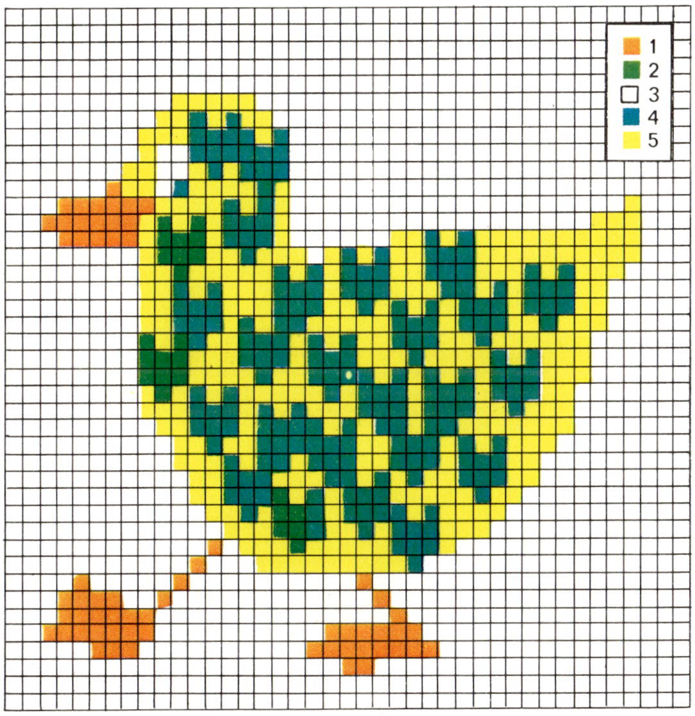

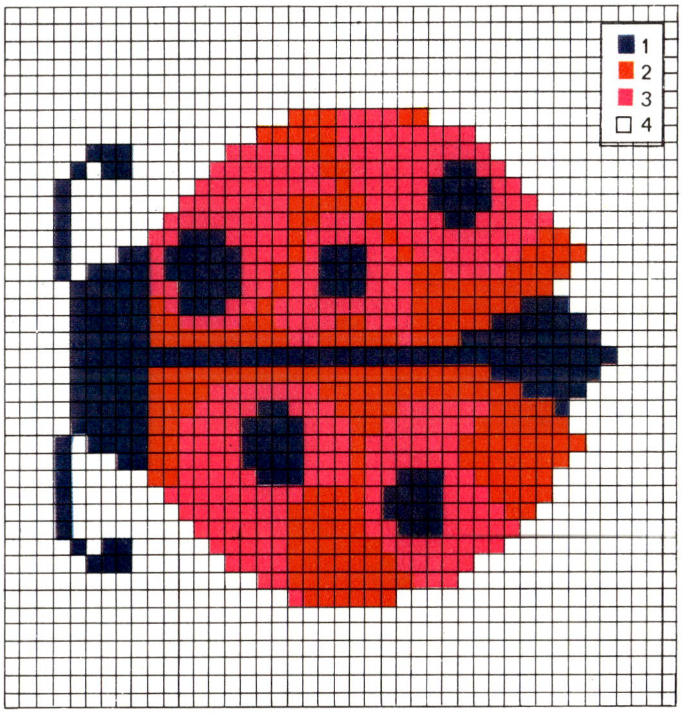

17-20

Four cheerful nursery cushions - ladybird, duckling, snail and kitten - worked in thick wool on canvas

Finished Measurement: 14″ square.
Fabric: For each cushion, single canvas, 10 threads to the inch, 18″ x 18″. Wool fabric for the backing, 17″ x 17″.
Threads: The number of skeins is in brackets after the colour number. D.M.C. Laine à Broder, 25 gramme skeins. **Ladybird. 1.** 7307(1) Navy blue; **2.** 7108(1) Red; **3.** 7204(1) Rose pink; **4.** (2) White. **Duckling. 1.** 7437(1) Orange; **2.** 7344(1) Green; **3.**(2) White; **4.** 7313(1) Blue; **5.** 7431(1) Yellow. **Snail. 1.** 7307(1) Navy blue; **2.** 7313(2) Blue; **3.**(2) White; **4.** 7344(1) Green. **Kitten. 1.** 7437(1) Orange; **2.** 7204(1) Rose pink; **3.** (2) White; **4.** 7344(1) Green; **5.** 7431(1) Yellow;
Needles: Rug or heavy embroidery.
Stitch: Cross.

Four amusing creatures decorate gay cushions for the nursery. Work them in thick, soft wool on canvas. The large cross stitches and simple colour schemes are quickly worked.

Oversew the edges of the canvas. Mark the centres and the area of the embroidery. Each stitch is worked over *three* threads of the canvas in each direction. Follow the chart carefully so that the animal is in the centre of the canvas square. Cross the stitches in the same direction throughout. Stretch and make up as shown on page 57.

21

Round blue and white cushion

Finished Measurement: 10″ diameter.
Fabric: White linen. Two squares 11″ x 11″.
Threads: Anchor Stranded Cotton. **1.** 0150. **2.** 0147. **3.** 0146. **4.** 0145.
Needles: Crewel, no. 7.
Stitches: French knot, long and short, satin and stem.

Transfer the design to the fabric as shown on page 54. Include the cutting and seam lines. Use two strands of cotton for the embroidery. Work one row of long and short stitch for the flowers. The long stitch slants toward the centre and leaves space for the French knot in the middle. Cut round the outer circle and cut another from the remaining square. Press and make up as shown on page 57. Couch six threads of blue over seam line as decorative finish.

22

Square blue and white cushion

Finished Measurement: $12\frac{1}{2}$″ x $12\frac{1}{2}$″.
Fabric: White linen. Two squares, 13″ x 13″.
Thread: Anchor Stranded Cotton. **1.** 0150(1 skein) **2.** 0147 (2 skeins).
Needles: Crewel no. 7. and no. 6.
Stitches: Stem and satin.

Trace the design onto the fabric as shown on page 54. Use three strands of cotton for the large motifs, two for the small. Work is satin stitch in the direction shown. The stem varies in width. Slant the needle diagonally to make the stem wider. With succeeding stitches, gradually straighten the needle to narrow the stem. At the centre of the large leaves, work a straight stitch over the vein. Press and make up as shown on page 57.

21

Round cushion

22

Square cushion

(chart overleaf)

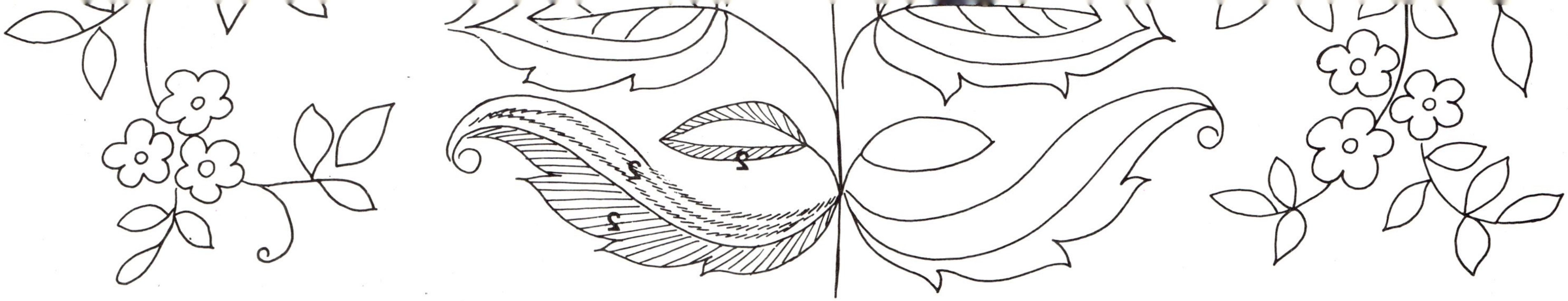

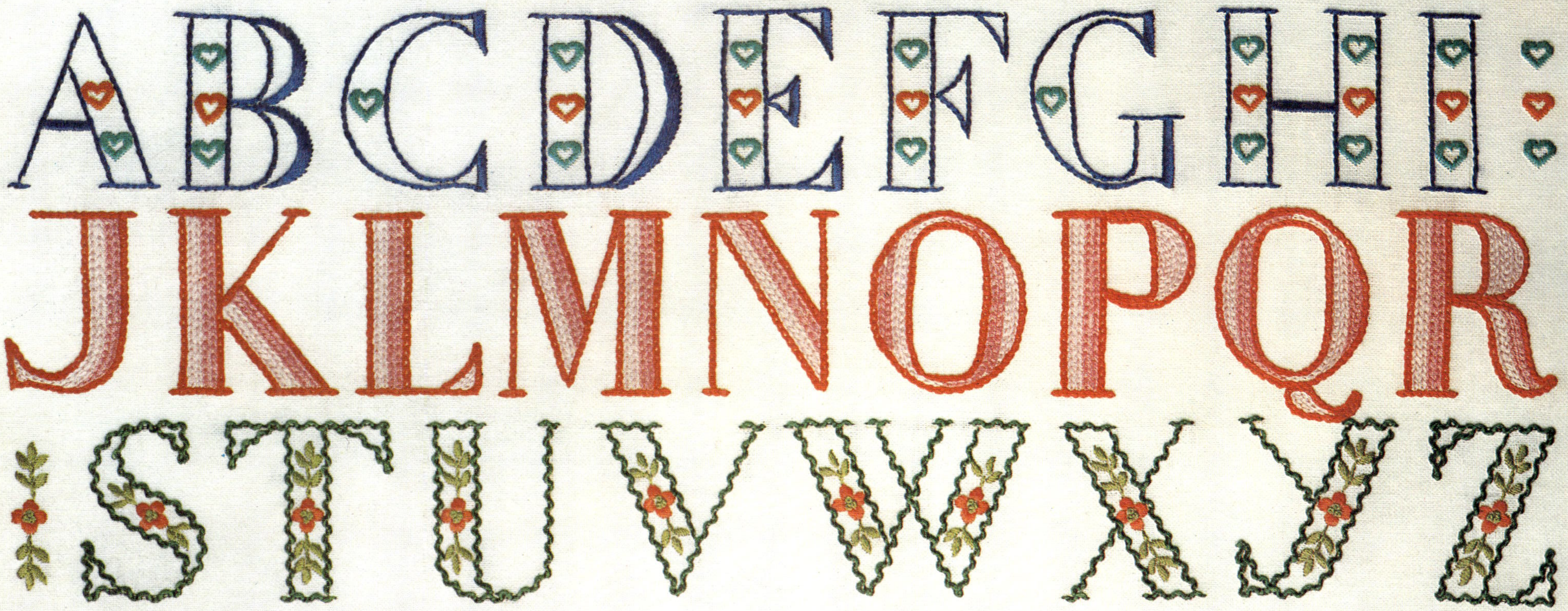

23

Alphabet - shown here embroidered in three styles - gay, formal and pretty

Threads: Stranded Cotton.
Needles: Crewel, no. 6. tapestry no. 22.
Stitches: A to I, stem and satin. J to R, chain, S to Z, threaded running, satin and French knots.

An alphabet of large letters with many uses. Three styles; gay, formal and pretty are shown here. Stitch them in your favourite colours and style to suit your personality.

Transfer the letter outline to the fabric as shown on page 54. Trace carefully to retain the clear shape of the letters. Work the outlines first. For the chain stitch letters, work as many rows of chain as will fit comfortably within the outline. Work the running stitches for threaded running exactly to the outline. Use the tapestry needle for threading. Thread loosely for the wavy effect. Work the satin stitch flowers and finally, the French knots. Vary the number of strands according to the fabric. Four strands will be needed for a dress weight linen. The finer the fabric the fewer the threads. Press as shown on page 55.

24

White flowers on an organdie mat

Finished Measurement: About 8½″ in diameter.
Fabric: White organdie 11½″ square. 1 yard bias binding.
Threads: Anchor Stranded Cotton. Three skeins of white 0402.
Needles: Crewel no. 7.
Stitches: French knots, long and short, threaded running.
A ring frame.

Flowers in two sizes are scattered across an organdie mat. The fine stitches appear to float in the transparent fabric but are not difficult to work.

Trace the design onto the fabric as shown on page 54. Include the circular hem-line but do not cut until the making up stage. Work the flowers in long and short stitch. Stitch from the outside, straight down the petal toward the centre. To work the flowers with a pierced centre take the final stitches down into the same hole. French knots form stamens at the larger flower centres. Outline the petals with threaded running stitch. Press and make up as shown on page 56.

25

Fragile pink water lily on an organdie mat

Finished Measurement: 8½″ diameter.
Fabric: White organdie 11½″ square. 1 yard pink bias binding.
Threads: 1 skein of each colour. Anchor Stranded cotton. **1.** 073 Pale old rose; **2.** 075 Old rose; **3.** 076 Dark old rose; **4.** 0295 Buttercup.
Needles: Crewel no. 7.
Stitches: French knots. Long and short, stem.
A ring frame.

Transfer the design to the fabric. Run a tacking line to mark the circular hemline. Do not cut out until the making up stage. With two strands of thread work the long and short stitches in the direction indicated in the trace pattern. Begin at the centre point of each petal and work toward the flower centre. Outline the petals with stem stitch using one strand of cotton. With two strands work the French knots over the completed embroidery. Press and make up as shown on page 56. Space French knots evenly rounded the bias bound edge of the mat.

26

Yellow butterflies on a scalloped mat

Finished Measurement: 9½″ diameter.
Fabric: White organdie, 12½″ square. 2 yards yellow bias binding.
Thread: 1 skein of each colour. Anchor Stranded Cotton. **1.** 0298 Buttercup yellow. **2.** 0360 Peat brown.
Needles: Crewel no. 7.
Stitches: French knots, stem, satin, straight.

Transfer the design to the fabric as shown on page 54. Include the scalloped hem line, but do not cut out. Stem stitch rows fill the upper wings. Use two strands of thread in the needle. Long, straight stitches are worked down and across the lower wings. The satin stitch bodies are worked with one thread and one thread stitches the long stitch of the antennae. A French knot is worked at the tip. Press and make up as shown on page 56.

27

Sweet pea spray border

Finished Measurement: About 10½″ square.
Fabric: White linen or organdie 13½″ square.
Thread: A skein of each colour. D.M.C. Stranded Cotton. **1.** 469 Olive green; **2.** 992 Blue green; **3.** 471 Light olive green; **4.** 309 Deep rose; **5.** 776 Pale rose; **6.** 604 Pale cyclamen; **7.** 603 Cyclamen; **8.** 470 Mid olive green.
Needles: Crewel no. 7.
Stitch: Long and short, stem, satin, threaded running.

Delicate sweet peas are worked in fine stitching as a pretty border for a mat.

Oversew the edges of the fabric and transfer the design as shown on page 54. The methods are the same for both the organdie and linen mat. For the organdie, fasten off the thread for each flower and leaf. A line of coloured thread across from one flower to another shows through at the front and blurs the design. Use two strands in the needle. The flowers are worked in long and short stitches, the buds and leaves in satin stitch. The stems are in stem stitch and the tendrils in threaded running. The design varies slightly in each section. Use colour 1. for the stems but vary the tones in the flowers and leaves. On the line indicated on the trace pattern, work a row of stem stitch in one of the greens as a hem decoration. Press and make up with a narrow, plain hem.

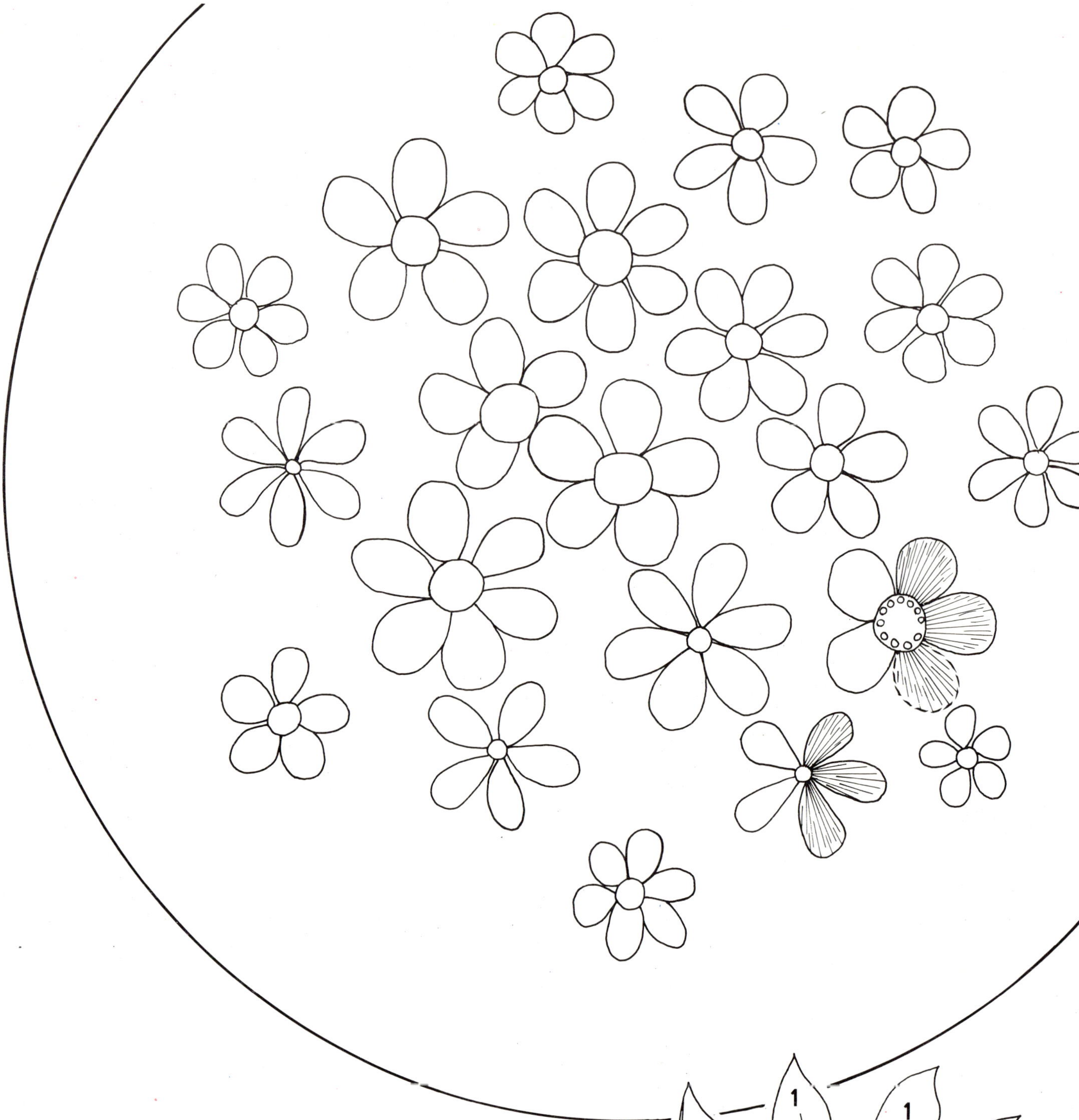

24 25

White flowers on organdie mat

Pink water lily mat

26

Mat with yellow butterflies

27

Sweet pea spray border

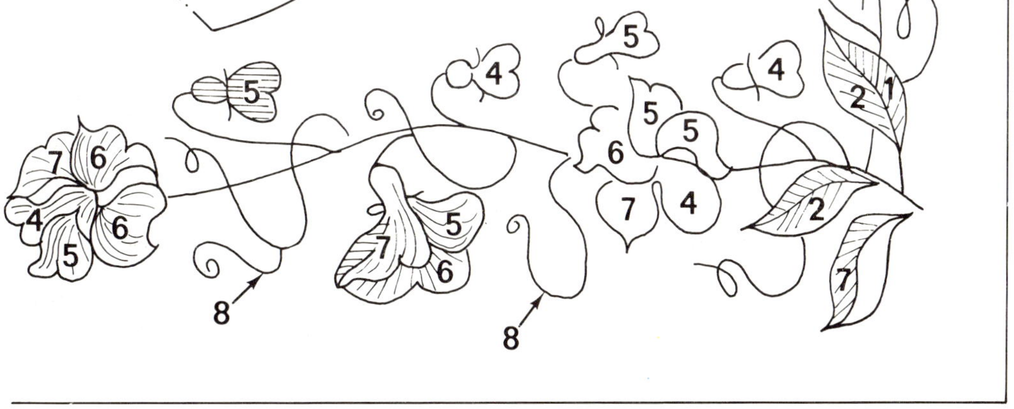

28-30

Richly coloured cushion in a patchwork of hexagonal shapes
(chart above)

Cushion with square motifs worked in cool tones
(chart overleaf)

Round cushion with a fan of triangular shaped motifs worked in warm tones on a cool background
(chart overleaf)

Finished Measurement: Hexagonal cushion, about 13″ x 11″. Square cushion, about 15″ x 15″. Round cushion, about 13″ diameter.
Fabric: Double canvas, 10 holes to the inch. Hexagonal cushion 17″ x 15″. Square cushion 19″ square. Round cushion 19″ square. Linen backing of the same size and bias binding and piping cord—2 yards for hexagonal and square cushion, 1½ yards for round cushion (optional).
Threads: Anchor Tapisserie wool. About one skein of each colour for each pattern motif. About 5 skeins off-white 0386 for the background for the round cushion.
Needle: Tapestry no. 18.
Stitch: Tent.

Three unusual cushions with a patchwork of patterns. The motifs can be worked with one skein of each of the colours. Warm tones combine in the rich colouring of the hexagonal cushion, cool tones for the square motifs on the square cushion. The round cushion combines the two themes. It has rich, warm colours thrown up by a cool ground colour. Sort your collection of threads into a similar range and have fun mixing those spare lengths into a wealth of pattern. The colour range is all-important and a large part of the pleasure of canvas work is in the colouring. Here is a chance to try out your own ideas.

For each cushion, mark the vertical and horizontal centres of the canvas. Begin at the centre motif and work outward. Avoid mistakes in counting by completing each motif before moving on to the next. The symbols on the charts denote separate colours. Stretch and make up as on page 57. The piping is optional.

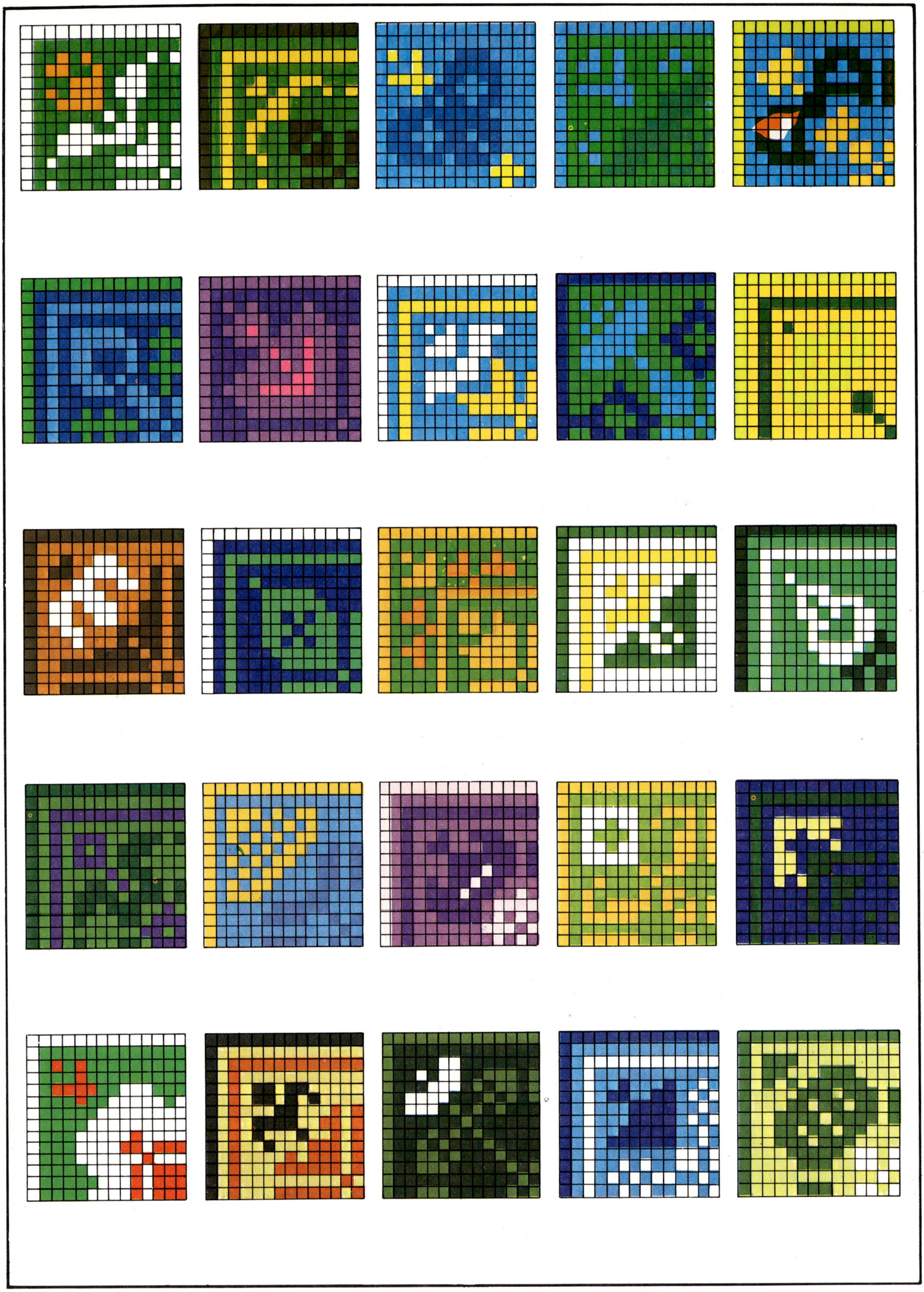

29

Canvaswork cushion in square motifs
(chart on left)

30

Cushion in triangular shaped motifs
(chart above)

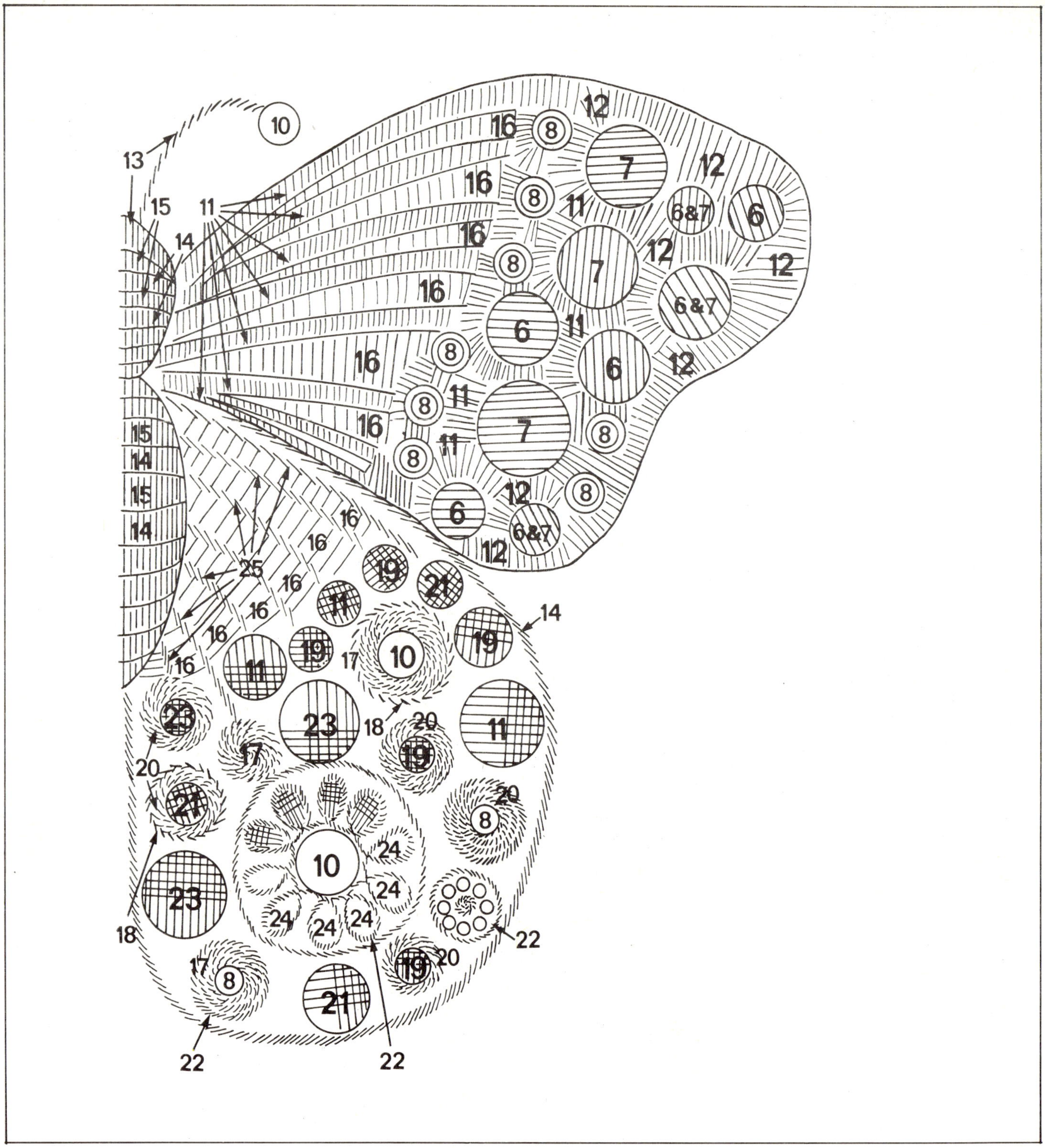

31

Yellow butterfly encrusted with pearls and golden stones

Finished Measurement: About 11″ x 10″ inner edge of frame as illustrated.
Fabric: Cream furnishing fabric with a slub weave, 14″ x 13″.
Threads: **1.** 3 skeins Antique gold thread O.O.E. 3-ply twist. 4 skeins of each of the following colours. D.M.C. Stranded cotton; **2.** 726 Pale gold yellow; **3.** 743 Mid gold yellow; **4.** 742 Dark gold yellow; **5.** 422 Fawn; **6.** 746 Gold white; **7.** 3033 Beige white; **Beads and jewels 8.** (20) large pearls; **9.** (17) small pearls; **10.** Gold stones (2 large, 2 medium, 2 small.) The following trace pattern numbers show combinations of the threads listed above.
11. 2 threads 1. 2 threads 3. 2 threads 5.
12. 2 threads 1. 2 threads 4. 1 thread 3. 1 of 5.
13. 3 threads 1. 3 threads 4. 2 threads 5.
14. 3 threads 1. 3 threads 3. 2 threads 5.
15. 1 thread 2. 2 threads 3. 1 thread 5.
16. Straight stitches worked with 1 thread 1.
17. Cord made with six threads 3.
18. 1 thread 3. 3 threads 1. 1 thread 4.
19. 2 threads 1. 2 threads 4. 2 threads 3.
20. 3 threads 1. 3 threads 3. Make into cord.
21. 2 threads 1. 2 threads 2. 1 thread 3.
22. 3 threads 1. 3 threads 3. 3 threads 5. Cord.
23. 2 threads 1. 2 threads 4. 1 thread 5.
24. 2 threads 2. 2 threads 3.
25. 3 threads 1. 1 thread 4. 2 threads 5. D.M.C. Soft Embroidery Twist—yellow.
Needles: Crewel no. 5., chenille no. 18.
Stitches: Satin, padded satin.
A slate frame.

Transfer the design to the fabric as shown on page 54. Mount the fabric in a frame as shown on page 54. A supported slate frame is needed so that both hands are free to apply the beads, jewels and cords. Use all six strands of thread in the needle unless otherwise specified. The satin stitch upper wings are worked with various blends of the colours listed. The outer edge of the wings, 12., is darker in tone than the inner, 11. Where two colour numbers are shown on the trace pattern—such as 6. and 7. in circles on the upper wing—use three strands of each colour in the needle together. Work the satin stitch circles after the lines of colour. Numbers from 11. to 25. on the trace pattern indicate the blends of colours for each area. Work the satin stitch on the lower wings and stitch the jewels and beads in place before applying the cords. Cords are made with lengths of the colours shown. Take an equal length of each colour. Fasten one end to a fixed point and twist at least fifty times. Fold in half and it will twist on itself into a light cord. Thread the cord into a chenille needle and take it through from the front to the back of the work. Stitch from the outside of a shape, to the inside. Thread a crewel needle with one strand of cotton and oversew the end of the cord securely to the back of the work. At the front, stitch into the twist of the cord so that the stitches are concealed and finish off by oversewing at the back before the unused length is cut. Work stem stitches with one strand of colour 1. round the large jewelled circle. Padded satin stitch circles are shown by crossed lines. Stitch vertically with soft embroidery cotton and horizontally with stranded cotton. Pack the top layer of stitches very closely. Finally work the satin stitch body and the stem stitch and jewelled antennae. Press face downward into a very thick, soft pad and stretch and make up for framing as shown on page 55.

32

Roses and rose leaves worked in satin stitch make a bold design for a mirror frame

Finished Measurement: 12″ x 9″.
Fabric: Cream linen 15″ x 12″.
Threads: The number of skeins needed are shown in brackets after the colour number. Anchor Stranded Cotton. **1.** 044(2) Carmine rose; **2.** 063(2) Magenta; **3.** 066(2) Raspberry; **4.** 0402(1) White; **5.** 0263(2) Dark almond green; **6.** 0261(2) Mid almond green; **7.** 0842(2) Light olive green.
Needles: Crewel no. 6.
Stitches: Long and short, satin and stem. Embroidery frame.
Cardboard, two pieces 12″ x 9″ for mounting.
Mirror 6″ x $4\frac{1}{2}$″.

Roses and satin stitch combine in a bold design for a mirror frame.

Oversew the edges of the linen and transfer the design as shown on page 54. Mark the outer and inner fold lines of the frame with tacking stitches. Stitch along the exact grain of the fabric. The leaves and flowers are worked in satin stitch the stalks in stem stitch. Use three strands of thread in the needle. Work from the outside of the flowers toward the centre. Work in long and short stitch for the larger petals, keeping to the angles shown on the trace pattern. Leave a very small space—a thread of fabric—between each petal. Stitch the leaves in the same way. Press and make up as shown on page 58.

33

Wall hanging in Moroccan style traditional embroidery

Finished Measurement: About 20″ x $16\frac{1}{2}$″.
Fabric: Double canvas, 5 holes to the inch. 24″ x 18″ width.
Thread: D.M.C. Laine à Broder, 25 gramme skeins. The number of skeins needed is in brackets after the colour number. **1.** (2) White; **2.** 7282(2) Light grey; **3.** 7207(3) Rose; **4.** 7110(2) Deep rose; **5.** 7314(4) Blue; **6.** 7469(6) Dark brown.
34 Large pearl beads.
Needles: Heavy embroidery or rug.
Stitch: Cross.

A Moroccan-style traditional embroidery adapted to make a striking modern wall hanging. The central motif is surrounded by border patterns of varying width and colour. Oversew the edges of the canvas. Mark the centres and the approximate area of the finished embroidery. Work in cross stitch over one pair of double threads in each direction. Note that the middle of the central motif is three stitches below the centre point of the canvas. When the cross stitch is complete, use a crewel needle and fine thread to sew the large pearls in the positions marked on the chart. Sew diagonally in the same direction as the cross stitch. Stretch and make up as shown on page 55.

34
Cornflower picture

35
Water lily picture

36

Pretty poppy picture

37

Marguerite picture

34-37

Four flower pictures - cornflower, water lily, poppy and marguerite

Finished Measurement: About 6½″ square inside frames.
Fabric: Evenweave linen, 20 threads to the inch. Four 9½″ squares.
Threads: 1 skein of each colour.

Cornflower Picture. Anchor Stranded Cotton. **1.** 0125 Indigo; **2.** 0117 Light Periwinkle; **3.** 0136 Cornflour blue; **4.** 0280 Muscat green; **5.** 0851 Dark blue green; **6.** 0218 Forest green; **7.** 0127 Dark indigo: **8.** 0132 Cobalt blue; **9.** 0118 Mid periwinkle; **10.** 0844 Olive green; **11.** 0268 Moss green; **12.** 0203 Apple green; **13.** 0186 Mid jade; **14.** 0259 Light almond green; **15.** 0896 Indian pink; **16.** 0104 Lilac; **17.** 0120 Light delphinium; **18.** 0158 Light kingfisher; **19.** 0185 Light jade;

Water Lily Picture. Anchor Stranded Cotton. **1.** 0259 Almond green; **2.** 0313 Mid tangerine; **3.** 0311 Light tangerine; **4.** 0203 Apple green; **5.** 0218 Dark forest green; **6.** 0281 Dark muscat green; **7.** 0301 Mid gorse yellow; **8.** 0323 Light orange; **9.** 0375 Snuff brown; **10.** 0299 Pale gorse yellow; **11.** 0376 Beige; **12.** 0306 Amber gold; **13.** 0337 Terra cotta; **14.** 0269 Dark moss green; **15.** 0297 Buttercup yellow; **16.** 0326 Orange.

Poppy Picture. D.M.C. Stranded Cotton. **1.** 733 light olive green; **2.** 992 Jade green; **3.** 986 Dark green; **4.** 954 Bright blue green; **5.** 321 Red; **6.** 335 Mid rose red; **7.** 581 Light olive green; **8.** 814 Deep red; **9.** Black; **10.** 776 Pale rose; **11.** 471 Light green; **12.** 304 Mid red; **13.** 894 Salmon pink; **14.** 904 Deep green; **15.** 317 Grey.

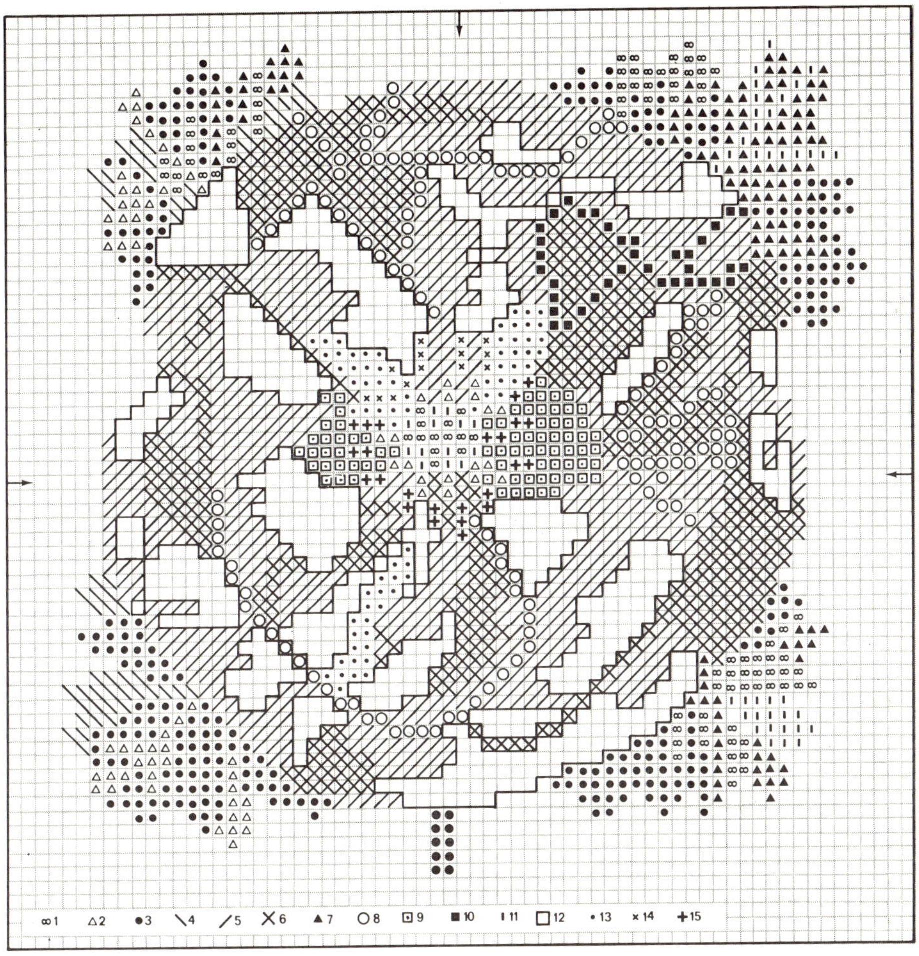

Marguerite Picture. Anchor Stranded Cotton. **1.** 049 Rose pink; **2.** 0281 Muscat green; **3.** 0855 Brown olive; **4.** 0242 Grass green; **5.** 0399 Grey; **6.** 0293 Buttercup yellow; **7.** 0189 Jade; **8.** 0264 Light moss green; **9.** 0307 Mid amber gold; **10.** 0397 Light grey; **11.** 0259 Light almond green; **12.** 0402 White; **13.** 0186 Jade; **14.** 0325 Orange; **15.** 0326 Dark orange; **16.** 0386 Cream; **17.** 0311 Tangerine.
Needle: Tapestry no. 22.
Stitch: Cross.
A ring frame.
Four picture frames, about 6½″ square inside frames.

The working method is the same for each panel. Oversew the edges to prevent fraying during working. Tack centre lines horizontally and vertically. Use four strands of thread in the needle. Work in cross stitch over two threads of the fabric in each direction. Begin at the centre of the flower and work outward in the varying groups of colour. An alternative method is to count the threads from the centre to the top of the design and work across in rows. Press the finished work and stretch onto boards for framing as shown on page 55.

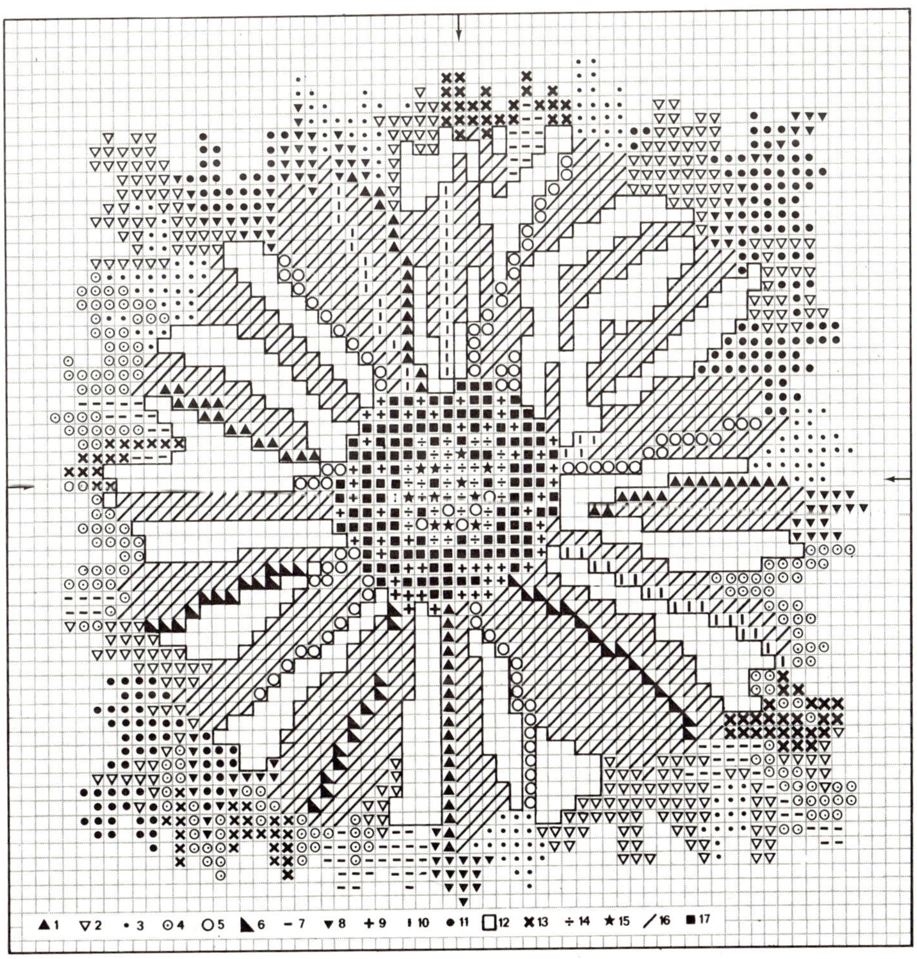

38 Curtain tie-back with bold flowers and strong colour contrast
39 Black, red and white spectacle case in surface stitchery
40 Formal border of stylised flowers, shown here decorating a candle holder
41 Two-way design for an attractive chair seat
42-45 Four different designs for jar tops in tent stitch
46 Embroidered flower spray to add charm to a cravat

38 Curtain tie-back

Finished Measurement: About 4½″ x 22″.
Fabric: Double canvas, 10 holes to the inch. 9″ x 26″. Lining 6″ x 26″.
Threads: D.M.C. Tapestry wool. The

number of skeins needed is shown in brackets after the colour number. **1.** (2) White; **2.** 7436(2) Orange; **3.** 7746(1) Pale yellow; **4.** 7727(1) Yellow/orange; **5.** 7946(1) Red; **6.** 7314(1) Pale blue; **7.** 7797(1) Blue; **8.** 7708(1) Violet; **9.** 7820(1) Dark blue; **10.** 7952(1) Light turquoise; **11.** 7956(1) Turquoise; **12.** 7595(1) Blue/green; **13.** 7549(1) Yellow/green; **14.** 7346 (4) Dark green (background).
Needles: Tapestry no. 18.
Stitch: Tent.
Three hooks and bars.

These bold flowers and strong colour contrast echo Victorian wool work. The curtain colour is picked out in the orange of the embroidery which makes a handsome foil to the plain curtains.

Mark the centre of the nine inch width of the canvas. Begin the embroidery two inches in from one end. Each square on the chart represents one stitch. The two arrows show the position of the repeat. Begin the embroidery at one end and continue for the length required. About three repeats will be needed for the twenty two inch length. Stretch the finished canvas and make up and line as shown on page 55. Stitch hooks and bars in position.

39 *Spectacle case in surface stitch*

Finished Measurement: About 8″ x 3½″.
Fabric: Double canvas 10 holes to the inch. 20″ x 7½″. Lining 18″ x 7½″. Vilene interlining 16″ x 3½″.
Thread: D.M.C. Coton Perle no. 3. in the following colours. **1.** Black; **2.** White; **3.** 666 Red. Two skeins of each colour.
Needle: Tapestry no. 20.
Stitch: Surface satin.
Spectacle case frame.

Black white and red and surface satin stitch combine to make a bold but simple design.

Oversew the edges of the canvas and mark the vertical and horizontal centres. Mark the area of the finished embroidery. The chart shows the order in which to use the colours and the angle of the stitches. Work with a double thread in the needle and stitch into the holes between each double pair of threads in the canvas. The single squared lines on the chart represent one pair of threads. Work the horizontal stitches across each block of colour.
Stretch and make up as shown on page 55.

40 *Formal flower border*

Finished Measurement: About 2½ x 18″.
Fabric: Double canvas, 10 holes to the inch, 6½″ x 22″.
Thread: D.M.C. Stranded Cotton. The number of skeins needed is given in brackets after the colour number. **1.** 3072(9) Grey; **2.** (15) Black; **3.** 307(2) Light gold; **4.** 972 (1) Gold; **5.** 946(2) Orange; **6.** 666(1) Red; **7.** 209(1) Light violet; **8.** 552(1) Violet; **9.** 799(2) Blue; **10.** 796(1) Dark blue; **11.** 472(3) Yellow/green; **12.** 702(2) Green.
Needles: Tapestry no. 20.
Stitch: Tent.
A slate frame.

Clear colours, off-set by black and grey combine in a border of stylised flowers. Here it is shown decorating a candle holder.

The arrows on the chart indicate one repeat which is one quarter of the candle holder border. Each square on the chart represents one stitch. Mark the horizontal centre of the canvas and work the design from the chart, using all six strands in the needle. Stretch and make up as shown on page 55.

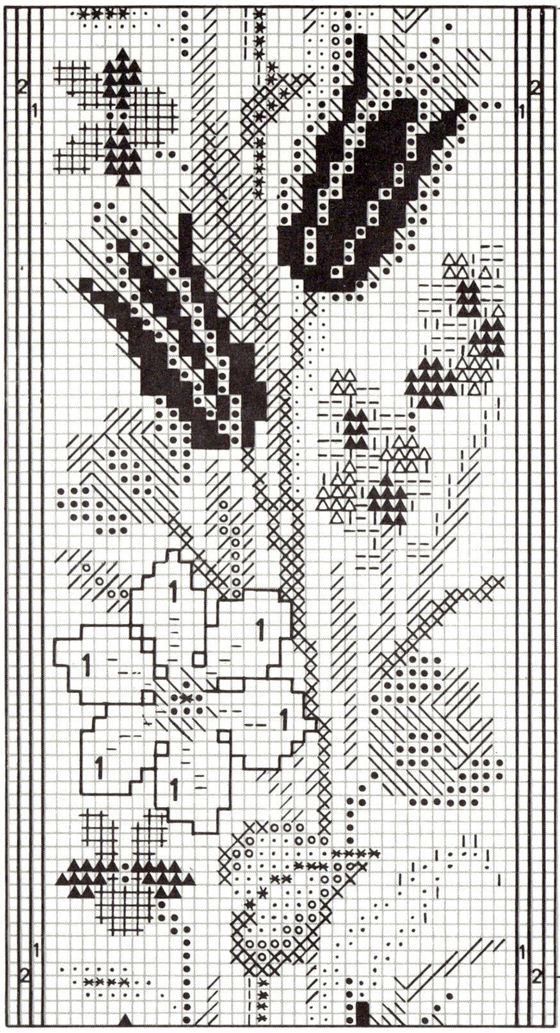

38

Symbol	Colour	Symbol	Colour
ı	1	+	8
\	2	▲	9
/	3	·	10
•	4	o	11
■	5	✱	12
−	6	×	13
△	7	□	14

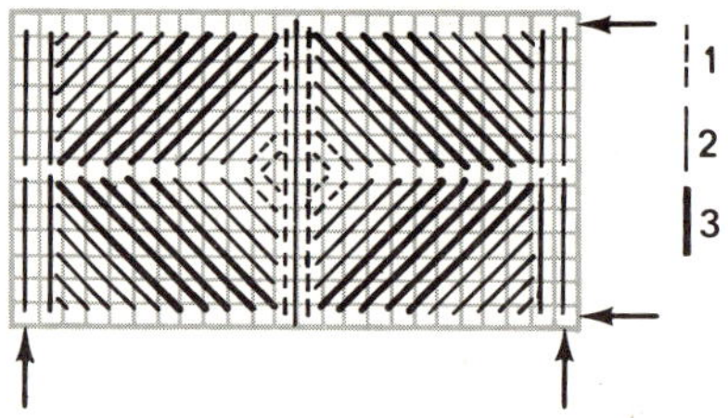

39

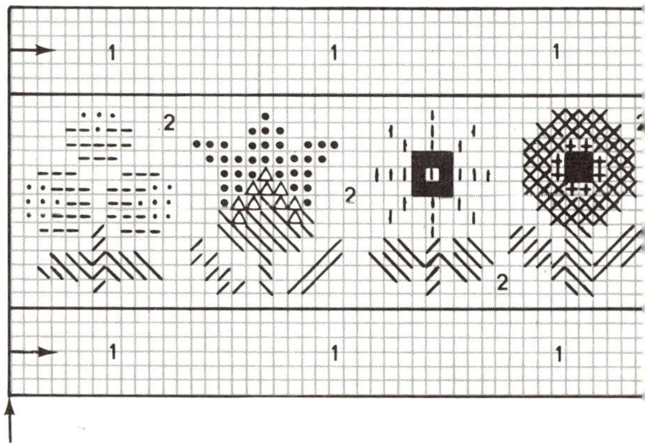

40

Symbol	Colour	Symbol	Colour
−	3	■	8
·	4	•	9
×	5	△	10
+	6	\	11
ı	7	/	12

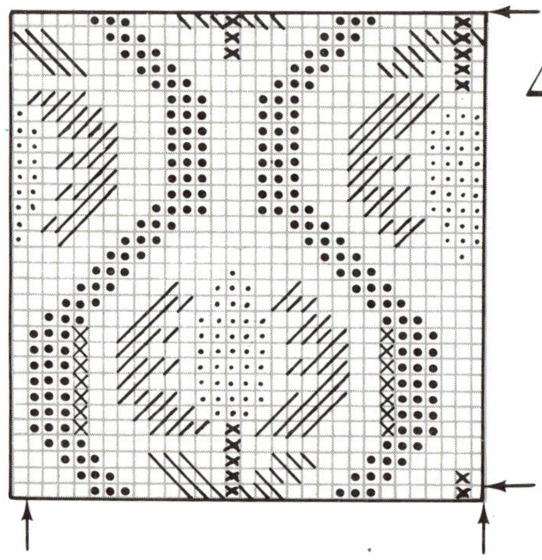

41

Symbol	Colour
·	1
/	2
•	3
×	4
\	5
□	6

41 *Two-way design for a chair seat*

Finished Measurement: About 18″ square.
Fabric: Double canvas, 10 holes to the inch. A 22″ square.
Threads: Anchor Tapisserie wool. The number of skeins needed is given in brackets after the colour number. **1.** 0335(2) Orange red; **2.** 019(3) Red; **3.** 0146(7) Blue; **4.** 0243(1) Light green; **5.** 0246(1) Dark green; **6.** 0386(12) Off white.
Needles: Tapestry no. 18.
Stitch: Tent.
A slate frame

Formal flowers and ogee stripes combine in an attractive two-way design with many uses. The neutral ground off-sets the clear colours. Used here as a chair seat in a modern setting, the embroidery would be equally effective with traditional furnishings. Measure the chair seat. Mark the centres of the canvas and outline the area of the seat. Make sure that the embroidery will cover the canvas well within the seat frame. Work diagonal tent stitch where there are large areas of one colour. For the small areas stitch in horizontal rows. Angle the stitches in the same direction throughout. Begin working at the centre front or back of the seat area. The centre stitch is marked with a circle on the chart. Each square of the chart represents one stitch. The pattern repeat is indicated by arrows. Follow on at the point indicated by the arrows and in the left corner.

Work repeats of the pattern across the chair seat. Continue upward until the marked area is filled. Stretch and make up as shown on page 57.

42-45 *Jar tops*

Finished Measurement: Jar tops, about $4\frac{1}{2}$″ diameter. Pill box about 2″ diameter.
Fabric: Double canvas, 10 holes to the inch. For each jar top, $8\frac{1}{2}$″ square. For the pill box 6″ square. A 17″ square of canvas is sufficient to work the four together. Braid trim: about $15\frac{1}{2}$″ length for each jar.
Threads: Anchor Stranded Cotton. The number of skeins is given in brackets after the colour number.
Design A: 1. 0289(1) Canary yellow; **2.** 0316(1) Tangerine; **3.** 0255(2) Parrot green; **4.** 0187(2) Jade; **5.** 072(12) Raspberry.
Design B: 1. 0161(2) Kingfisher; **2.** 0132 (1) Cobalt; **3.** 0170(2) Peacock blue; **4.** 0112(1) Parma violet; **5.** 0402(12) White.
Design C: 1. 037(2) Light blossom pink;

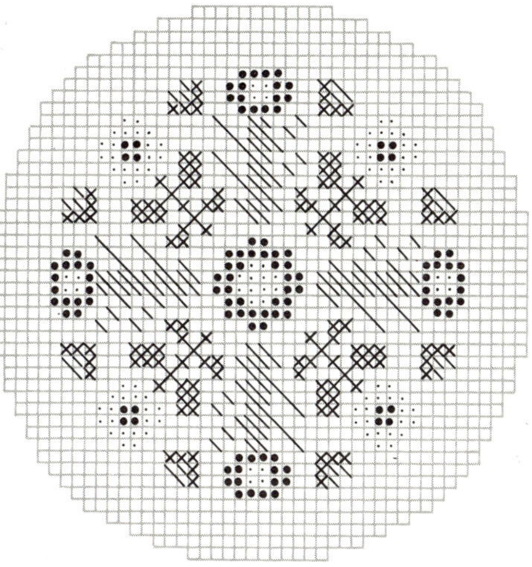

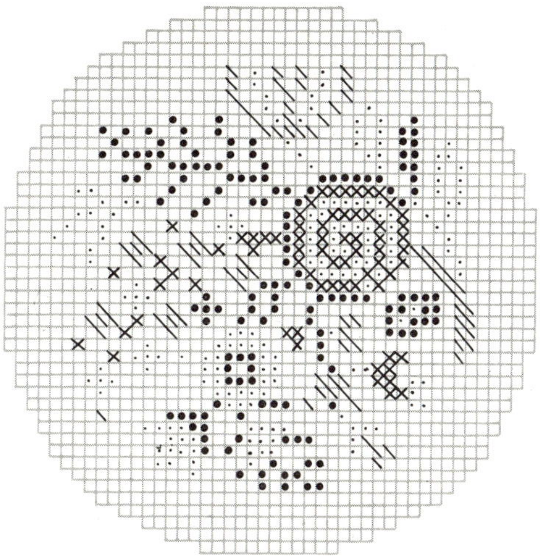

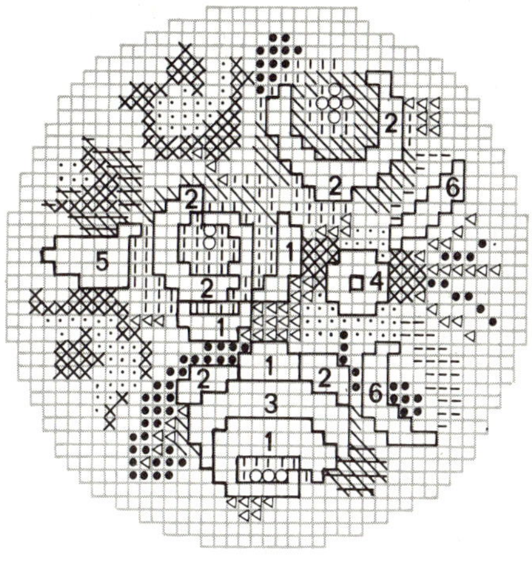

42-45

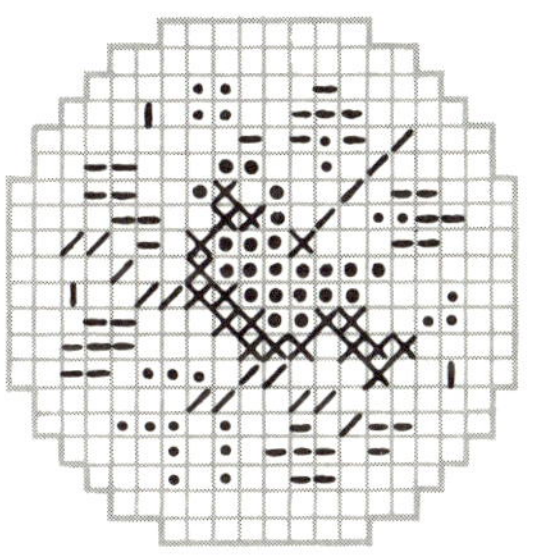

46

2. 038(1) Mid blossom pink; **3.** 039(2) Dark blossom pink; **4.** 0131(1) Dark cobalt blue; **5.** 0243(1) Grass green; **6.** 0109(1) Parma violet; **7.** 047(1) Turkey red; **8.** 0128(1) Light cobalt blue; **9.** 0130(1) Mid cobalt blue; **10.** 0256(1) Parrot green; **11.** 098(1) Violet; **12.** 0293(5) Buttercup.
Design D: 1. 0168(1) Peacock blue; **2.** 046(1) Scarlet; **3.** 0340(1) Terra cotta; **4.** 0380(1) Coffee; **5.** 0281(1) Muscat green; **6.** 0244(1) Grass green; **7.** 0259(2) Pale almond green.
Needles: Tapestry, no. 20.
Stitch: Tent.
Fabric glue. Slate frame.
Thin card. For each jar a circle 4½″ diameter. For the pill box 2″ diameter.

Four different designs and three sizes worked in simple tent stitch to decorate jar lids.

Mark the centres of the canvas in each direction. Each square on the chart represents one tent stitch. Work the design from the centre outward. Where only one or two stitches of a colour are to be worked, carry the thread across the back of the canvas to the next position for the colour. Let the thread lie loosely so that the canvas is not pulled out of shape. Subsequent stitches will cover the loose thread at the back. Stretch and make up as on page 57.

46 *Flower spray for a cravat*

Finished Measurement: A bought square scarf in fine wool. About 26″ square.
Threads: Anchor Stranded cotton, one skein of each colour. **1.** 0185 Jade; **2.** 0204 Apple green; **3.** 0132 Cobalt blue; **4.** 0402 White; **5.** 0315 Tangerine.
Needles: Crewel no. 7.
Stitches: Buttonhole, French knots, satin, stem, straight.
A ring frame.

A plain scarf with the individual touch of an embroidered spray. Colour numbers are given, but as the embroidery takes only a small amount of thread you may like to experiment with threads left from other projects. White is used here for contrast. There are two greens in soft tones and two strong colours, blue and tangerine.

Using the tissue paper method, transfer the design to the fabric. The stitches are indicated in the trace pattern. Work buttonhole stitch for the solid flowers and straight stitches for the spiky flowers. Angle them toward the centre point. Lastly, work the satin flower centres. Finish by pressing lightly face down into a thick pad.

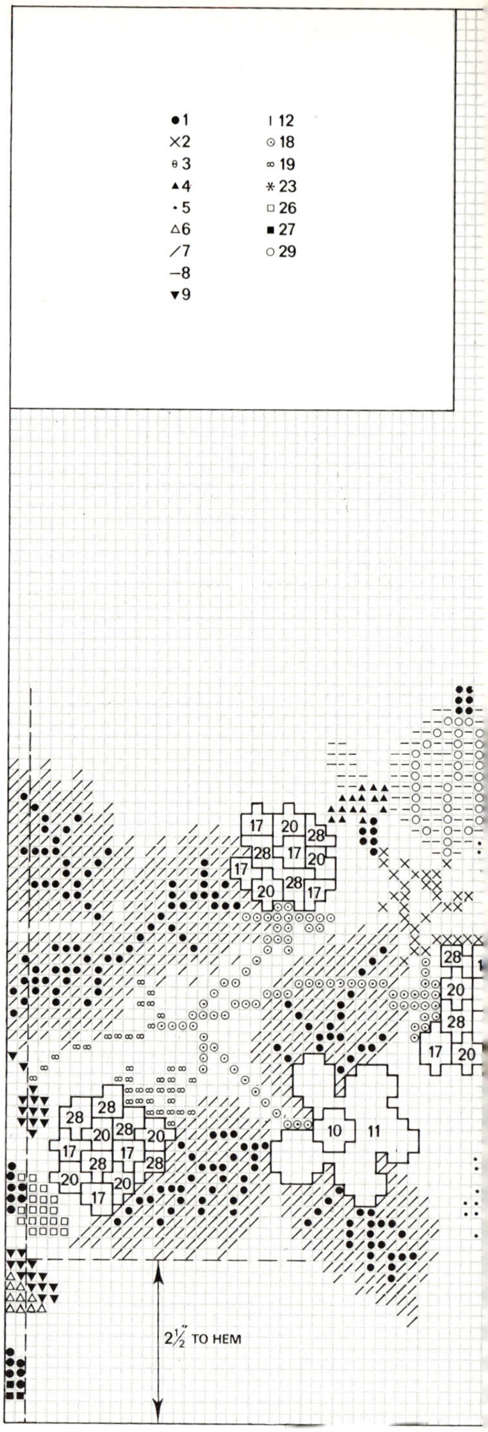

47 Flowers and fruits in fine cross stitch around a circular tablecloth
48 Bold cow parsley wall hanging with richly textured cross stitch florets.

47 Circular tablecloth embroidered with fruits and flowers

Finished Measurement: 54″ diameter.
Fabric: Evenweave linen, 20 threads to the inch. 55″ x 55″.

Threads: Figures in brackets show the number of skeins of each colour. Anchor Stranded cotton. Use four strands of cotton, except for number 15, where 5 strands are used. **1.** 0269(4) Dark moss green; **2.** 0265 (2) Light moss green; **3.** 0259(2) Light almond green; **4.** 0254(5) Light parrot green; **5.** 0256(16) Mid parrot green; **6.** 0258(5) Dark parrot green; **7.** 0243(16) Mid grass green; **8.** 0278(3) Light muscat green; **9.** 0217(2) Dark forest green; **10.** 0297(1) Buttercup yellow; **11.** 048(1) Pale rose pink; **12.** 0349(1) Mid chestnut; **13.** 019(5) Light cardinal red; **14.** 021(2) Deep cardinal red; **15.** 0132(3) Mid cobalt blue; **16.** 0129(2) Light cobalt blue; **17.** 0119(2) Dark periwinkle; 0402(3) White. See numbers 25 and 30. Numbers 18 to 30 are mixed strands from the colours shown above. 18 to 27, use two strands of each colour. 28 to 30, three strands of the first colour number and one of the second. **18.** 7-1; **19.** 9-1; **20.** 16-17; **21.** 8-3; **22.** 13-3; **23.** 1-15; **24.** 13:3; **25.** 0402 White-11; **26.** 1-12; **27.** 5-12; **28.** 15-17; **29.** 2-1; **30.** 0402 White-11.

Needles: Tapestry no. 22.

Stitch: Cross.

Light yellow bias binding.

Flowers and fruits in fine cross stitch surround a circular cloth. The closely worked cross stitch adds weight to the linen in a richly coloured border.

Oversew the edges of the fabric to prevent fraying. Run a tacking thread to mark the vertical and horizontal centres. Begin the embroidery at the chart centre line and match to the centre line of the linen. Begin at the marked point two and a half inches in from the edge. The chart section shown is one eighth of the complete circle. Complete each area before moving on to the next. Count carefully and check that you have the pattern correct. Work in cross stitch over two threads of the fabric. When four sections, half the cloth, are complete the embroidery should have reached the opposite centre line. When the embroidery is complete, press as explained on page 55. Draw a circular cutting line as explained on page 55. Work on the wrong side of the cloth. Machine stay-stitch along the line before cutting. Finish with bias binding.

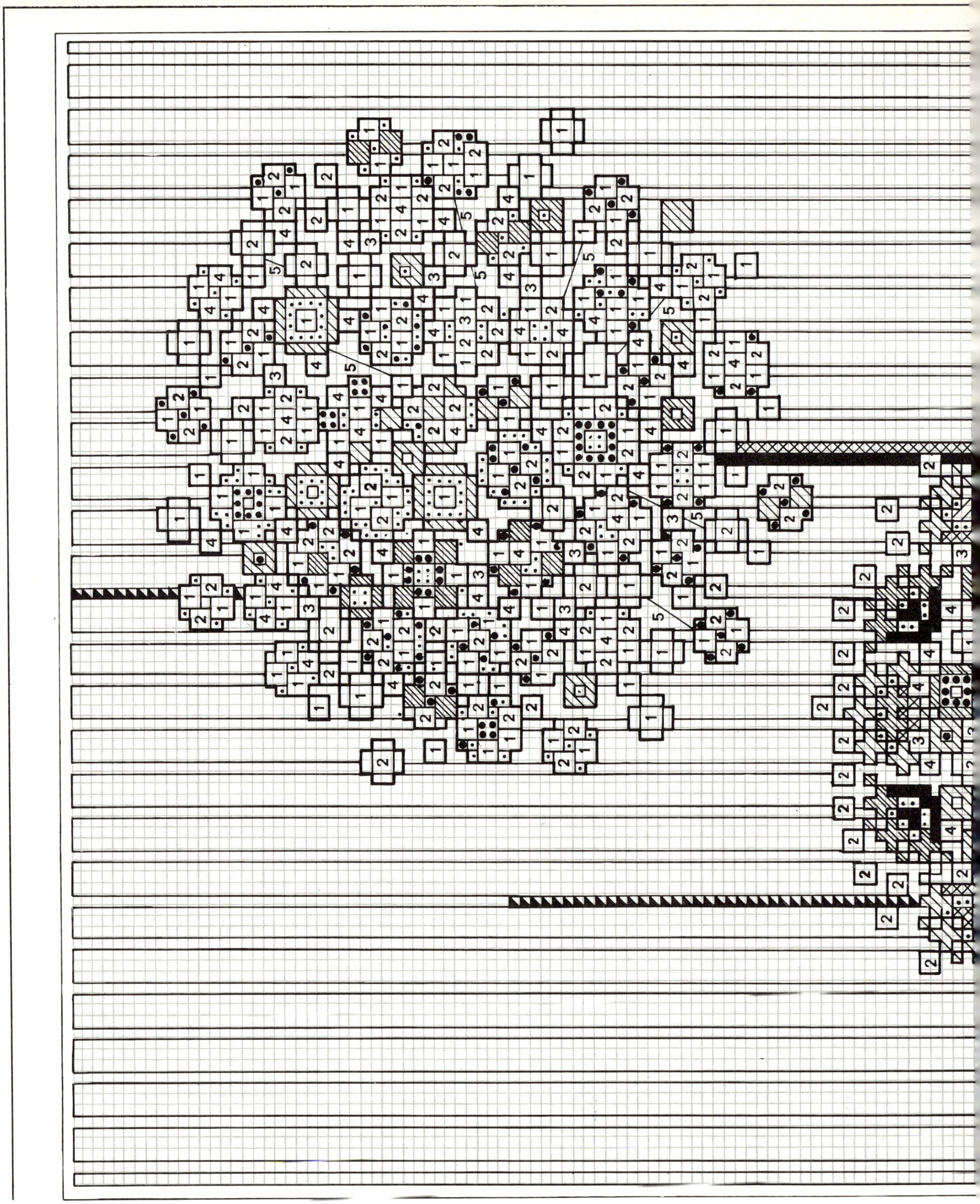

48 *Richly textured cow parsley design for a wall hanging*

Finished Measurement: 16½″ x 10½″.
Fabric: Double canvas, 10 holes to the inch, yellow or white. 20½″ x 14″.
Thread: The number of skeins required is shown in brackets after the colour number. Appleton's tapestry wool. **1.** 991(2) White; **2.** 851(2) Custard yellow; **3.** 0402(1) White Anchor Stranded Cotton; **4.** 472(2) Light Autumn yellow; **5.** 298(1) Dark Jacobean green; **6.** 407(1) Dark sea green; **7.** 427(1) Mid leaf green; **8.** 406(1) Sea green; **9.** 545 (14) Early English green; **10.** 563(2) Mid sky blue; **11.** 251(2) Grass green; **12.** 434 (1) Mid signal green.
Needles: Tapestry no. 18.
Stitches: Cross and double cross.
12″ wooden batten, about 1½″ wide.
Webbing, 11″ long, 2″ wide.

Hedgerow flowers make a bold design for a hanging. These myriad florets are stitched with single and double cross stitches. The resulting texture is a delight to look at and the stitches are fascinating to work.

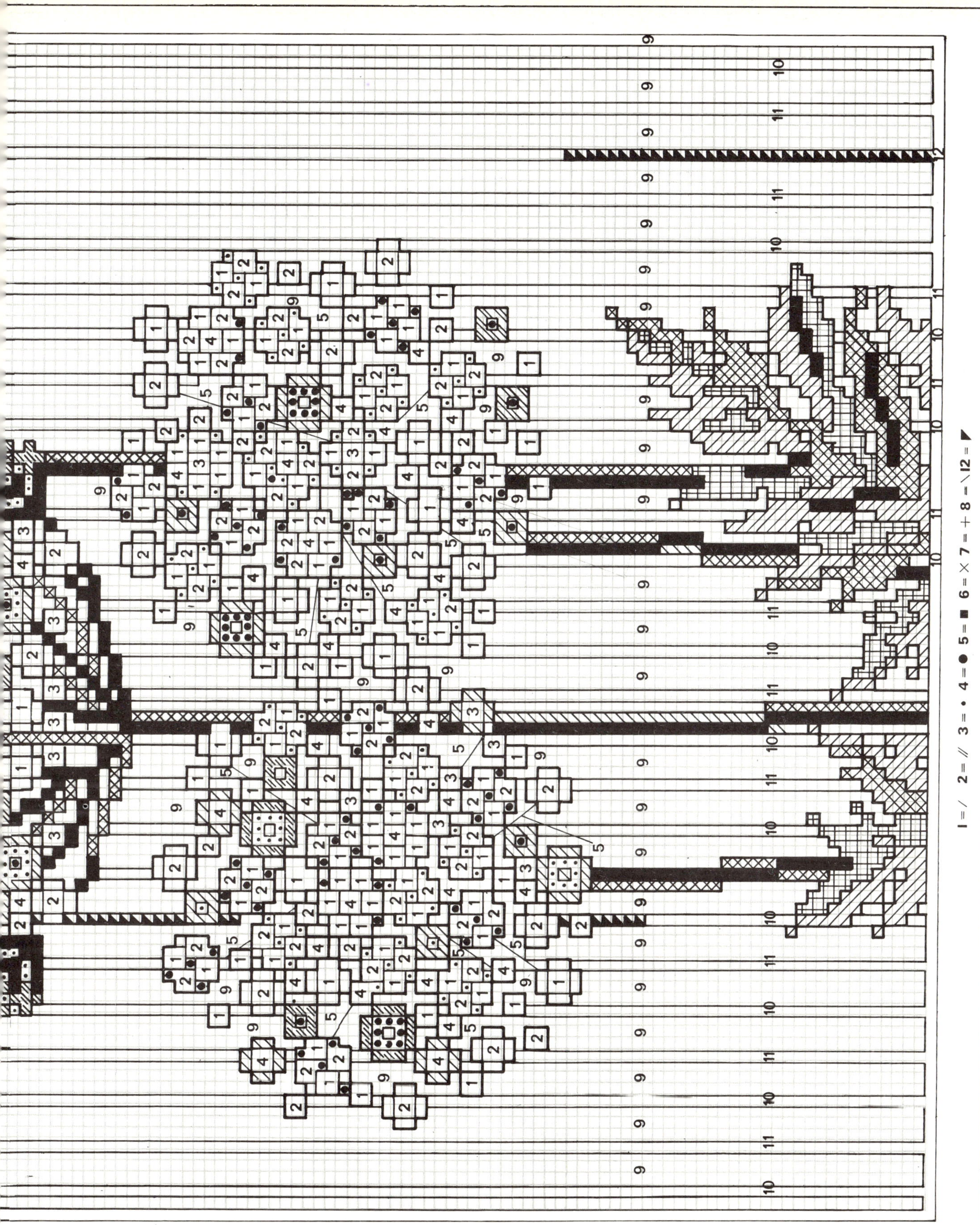

Oversew the edges of the canvas to prevent fraying.

Mark the vertical and horizontal centres and the area of the embroidery. Count from the top centre of the chart and begin by working the large, top flower. All the flowers are worked by the same method. The large, double cross stitches are taken over two pairs of threads in each direction. The single cross stitches over one pair of threads in each direction. These two stitches are intermixed over the flower head. A figure denotes a double cross stitch, a symbol, a single cross stitch. Figure 1. for example denotes white wool and a double cross stitch. Symbol '/' denotes white wool and a single cross stitch. Some of the squares show neither figure nor symbol. Here the canvas is left uncovered, adding to the texture interest of the hanging. The leaves and stems are in single cross stitch. When the flowers are complete, take a long stitch of colour 5. across the flower heads as shown on the chart. Couch this fine 'stem' in position with a pointed needle threaded with a fine, matching thread. Work the background cross stitch. Work in rows along the length of the canvas for rhythmic and quick stitching. Stretch and make up as shown on page 55.

embroidery know-how

Enlarging a design

With a ruler and pencil, enclose the outline drawing in a square or rectangle. Draw centre lines horizontally and vertically, divide these again, and draw a separate rectangle to the size required and divide in the same manner. Copy the outlines from the smaller to the larger squares. Letters and figures help to identify the squares.

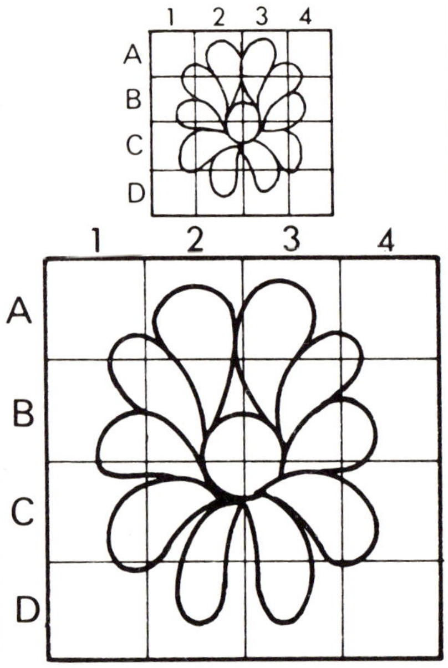

To prepare the fabric

Oversew the edges of the fabric to prevent fraying during working.

To work from a chart

With running stitch, mark the centres of the linen or canvas. Each square on the chart represents a stitch. Follow the pattern on the chart and work each stitch on to the canvas. When working in cross stitch, begin at one end and work the design and background in rows. To begin, work a few stitches, leaving a length of thread on the surface. Thread into the back of the worked stitches, and fasten off in the same way. Or, where possible, bring the thread to the front of the canvas and leave. The next stitches will cover the loose thread left at the back, and the thread at the front is cut off.

To trace the drawn outline

Tack horizontal and vertical centre lines on to the fabric. Trace the given outline on to tissue paper, mark the centres, and pin the tracing into position on the fabric. Use the tacked lines as a guide. With running stitch and one strand of cotton, outline the design. Use the colour of the finished embroidery. A smaller stitch on the surface than underneath allows for the easy removal of the tissue paper. Remove the pins and tear the paper away carefully. Round-ended tweezers are useful for pulling off any fragments of tissue paper caught in the stitches. The guide lines and colours are laid out clearly on the fabric and they become part of the embroidery and need not be removed when the work is finished. For organdie: draw the traced line on to the tissue paper with a pen. Pin to the BACK of the organdie. The design can be seen through the fabric and outlined with running stitch. There is no need to pierce the paper.

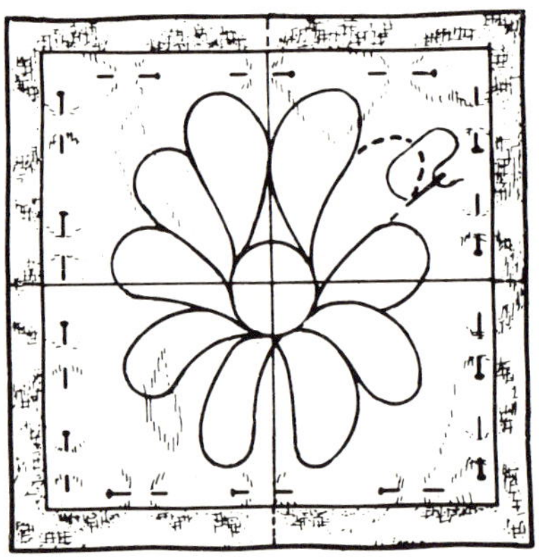

Embroidery frames

A frame is helpful for the even working of some techniques. There are two basic types, the ring and the slate frame.

The ring frame. It consists of an inner and an outer ring, the outer has an adjustable screw, and the fabric is gripped taut between the two rings. Easily positioned and removed it is useful for working on a large area and is also useful when an embroidery has a variety of stitches, some of which may be worked more easily in and some out of the frame.

Rings with a screw clamp for fixing to the table, or with a stand, are the most useful as they leave both hands free for working.

To mount the fabric: separate the inner and outer rings, and place the fabric over the inner ring. A square of tissue paper will prevent the rings marking the fabric. Push the outer ring into position, and tear away the centre of the tissue paper and tighten the ring screw. To avoid stretching the fabric, ensure that the weave lies vertical and horizontal.

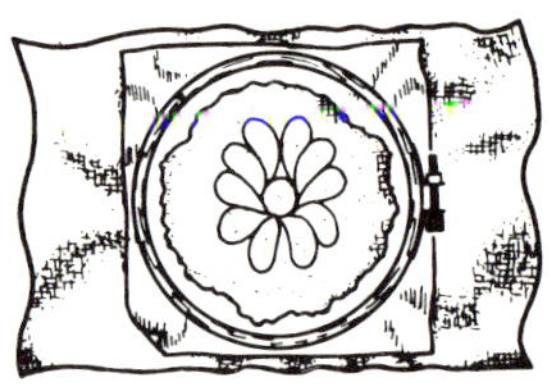

The slate frame. This holds the whole area of the fabric firmly and is obtainable in several sizes from 18″ wide.

When the fabric is mounted, support the frame between two tables or a table and chair. Both hands should be free to work, one above and one below the fabric. The diagram shows how to mount the fabric. Mark the centres of the webbing at each end of the frame, make a single turning at each end of the fabric to be mounted and mark the centre. Place the centres right sides together and oversew fabric to frame. Begin at the centre and work outward, and repeat at the opposite end. Insert the side slats and fix in position

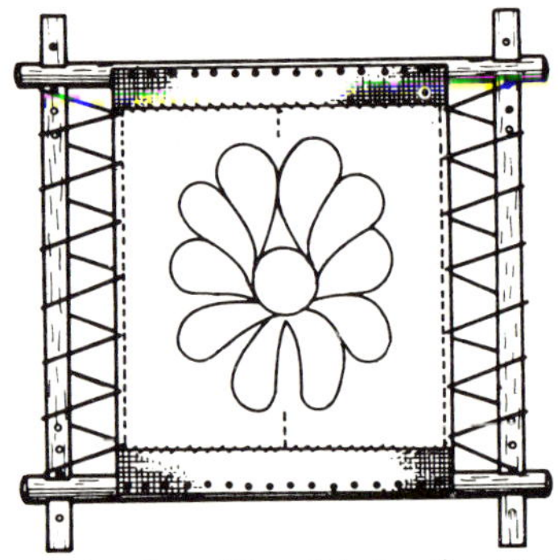

with split pins. The fabric should be taut, but not strained. Tack a hem along the sides, laying in a piece of string to strengthen it. Begin at the centre and, with a packing needle and fine string, lace the side of the fabric to the side supports. Tighten evenly at each side and knot the string firmly.

Pressing and stretching

To press embroidery – pad a large, flat surface with a blanket and ironing cloth. Lay the embroidery face downward and press with a damp cloth.
To stretch canvas work – pad a board with clean, damp blotting paper. Place the canvas work face upward on the blotting paper, and starting at the centre fix one end of the canvas with drawing pins. Align the horizontal threads with the edge of the board. Repeat at the opposite end and at the sides. Leave to dry for at least twenty four hours.

To prepare embroidery for a picture frame

Cut a piece of cardboard or hardboard to fit the frame, mark centres and match with the embroidery. Turn the edges of the fabric over the card and stitch firmly in place with strong thread. Start from the centre and work outward. Tighten the thread so that there is an even pull on the fabric and fasten off securely, and repeat for the two remaining sides. When choosing a frame allow sufficient depth to prevent the embroidery pressing on the glass. Embroidery shows to best advantage unglazed.

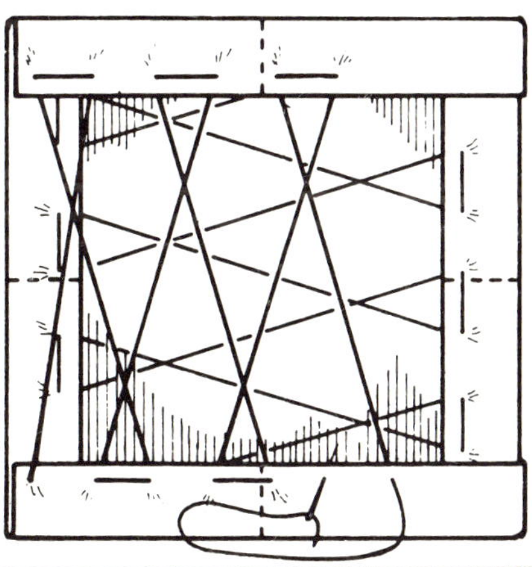

Making up with an interlining

(Belt, spectacle case, shopping bag and handbag etc.) The basic method is the same for each.
Cut interlining, eg Vilene, to fit within the hem lines. Lay the decorated fabric face downward and pin the interlining in

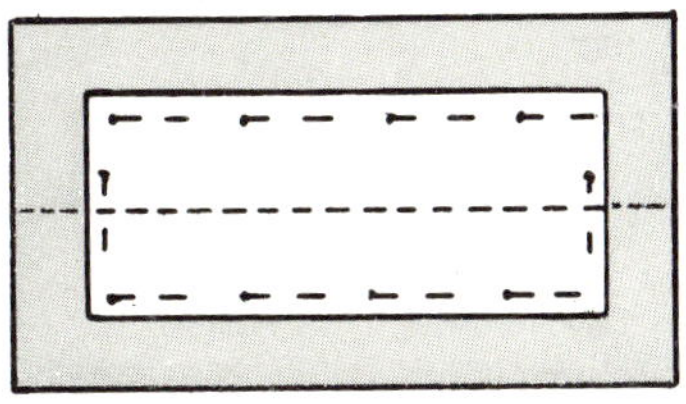

position. Snip at the corner as shown so that the fabric lies flat. With open herringbone, stitch the seam allowance to the interlining, cut a lining the same

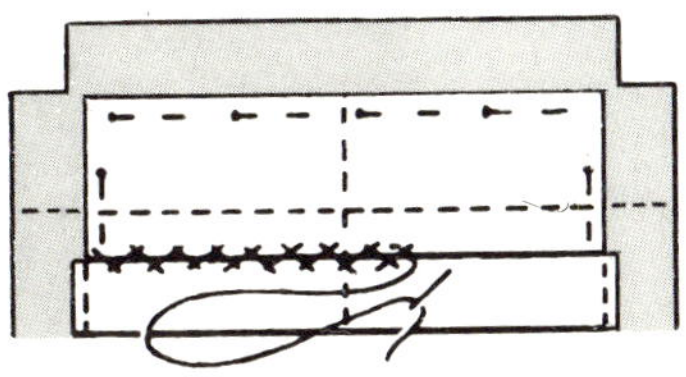

size as the decorated fabric, turn in slightly more than the seam allowance and slip stitch into position.

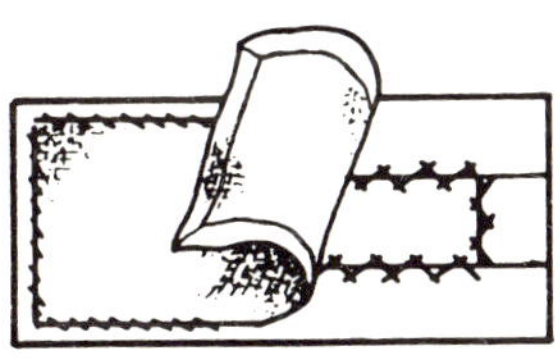

Mounting a spectacle case into a metal frame

Follow the interlining and lining instructions. Measure the side opening of the metal frame and mark the measurement onto the embroidery. Oversew the side seam as far as the opening. Fit the embroidery to the inside of the frame and with a strong thread oversew through the punched holes.

Marking circular cloths and mats

Measure and mark the centre of the fabric. Cut a length of string, measuring from the centre to the required extent of the circumference. Fasten a pencil at one end and a drawing pin at the other, fix the drawing pin at the centre mark and draw the circle, keeping the string taut.

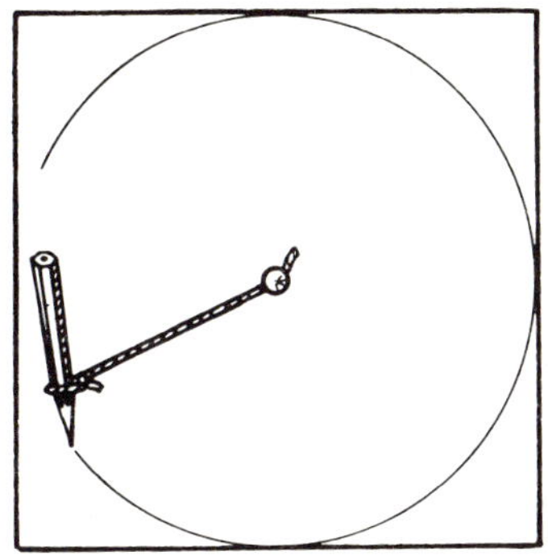

For a small circle, cut a strip of card, at one end make a hole for the pencil point and at the other fix a drawing pin. It may be used in the same way as the string and will accurately repeat a series of mats of the same size.

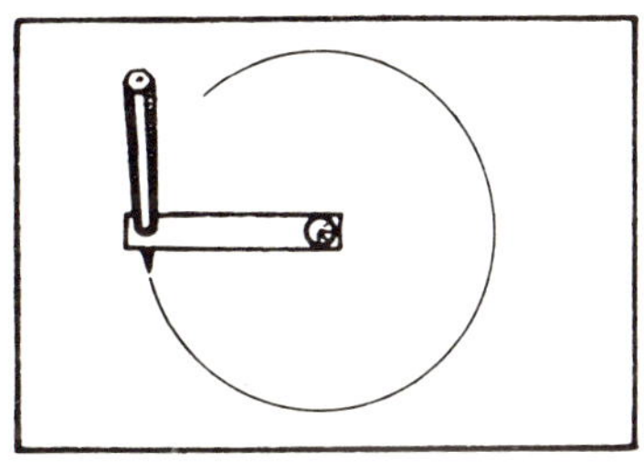

Joining the fabric for a large cloth. If the fabric has to be joined, stitch the seam and press open before marking the circle. Two side seams are less conspicuous and the circle may be cut from slightly less fabric if two side seams are stitched. Cut the length required, and divide the remaining piece down the centre. Match centres of each piece and join the two half pieces, one each side of the whole. Press seam open, mark the circle as shown, and cut the circle and stitch the hem when the embroidery is complete.

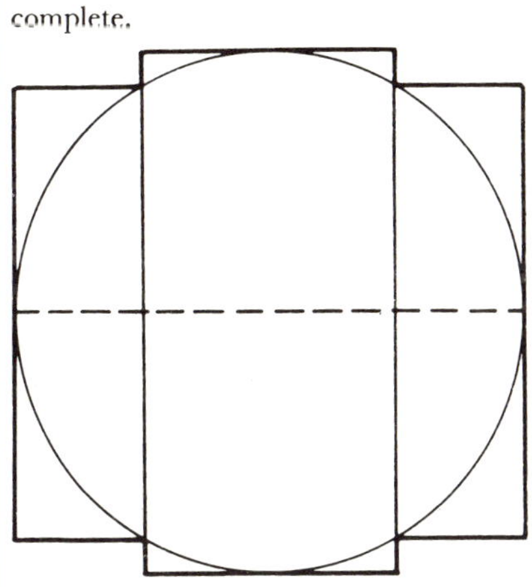

Finishing methods suitable for tablecloths, mats and bedspreads

An allowance of approximately 1½ inches has been made on the fabric amounts given which allows for mounting in an embroidery frame and for stretching. Some of this allowance may need to be cut when making up. Hems should relate in size to the weight of the fabric – a smaller hem for lightweight than for heavy. On a fabric which frays easily make the first turning wider than normal.

Mitred corner and plain hem. Fold and press the hem, open out and fold the corner on the inner fold line, and cut off the corner, leaving a seam allowance. Refold the hem, slipstitch the mitre and continue hemming.

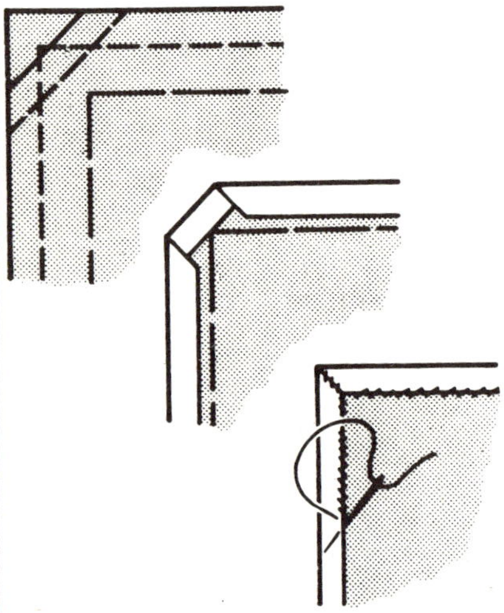

Fringe trimming. Pin the heading of the trimming to the hem line and machine or hand stitch firmly in place.

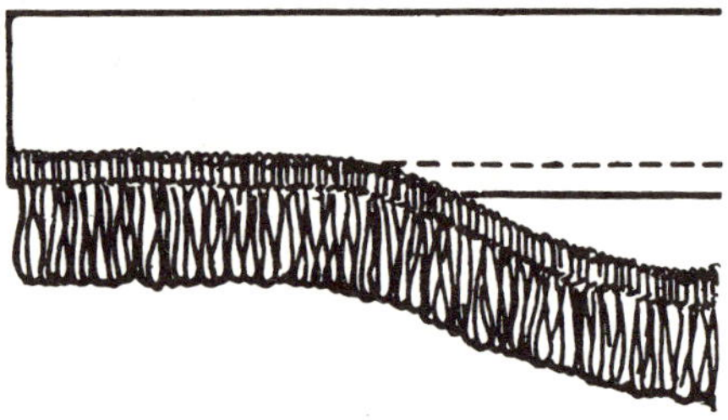

Finishing a curve. Before cutting the curve, run a gathering thread within the cutting line. Cut the curve and pull the

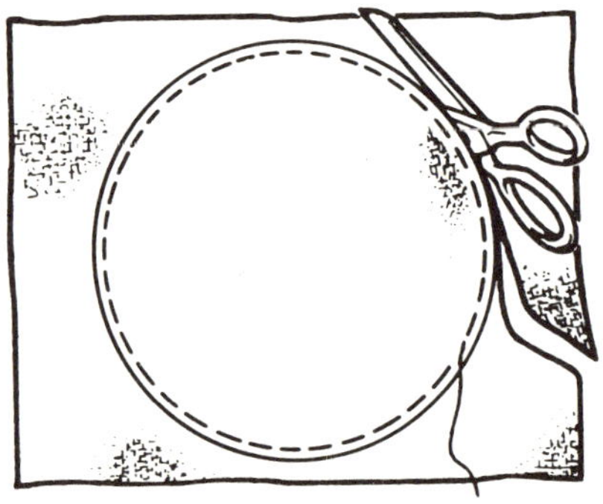

gathering thread slightly to take in the extra fabric on the turning. Fold, press and stitch the hem in the usual way.

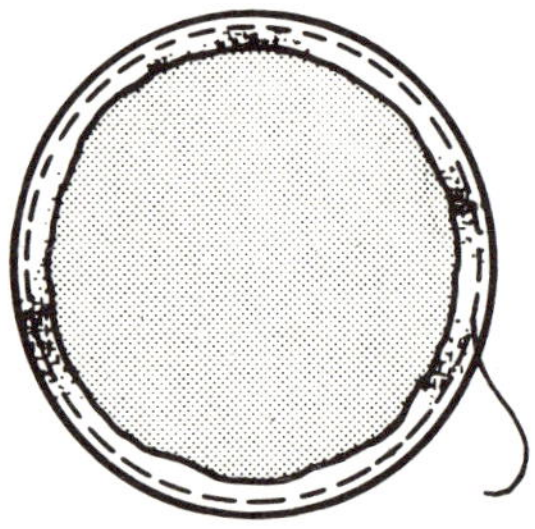

Binding a hem For a concealed hem: place bias binding and the finished embroidery right sides together and mach-

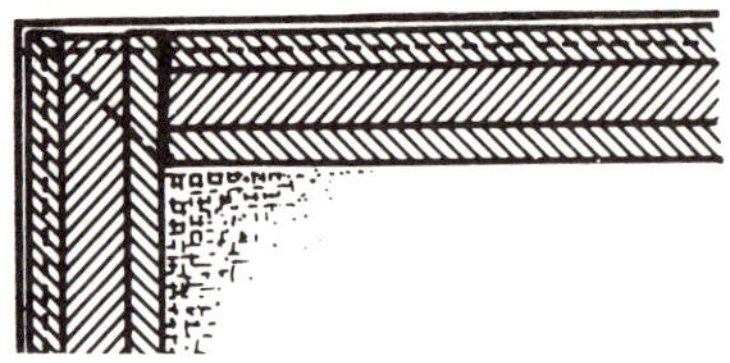

ine stitch. Fold in the binding for a neat corner. Turn to the wrong side of the fabric and slipstitch by hand. As a decorative finish (suitable for lightweight fabrics) fold the binding in half and tack over the edge of the fabric. Back stitch by hand or machine stitch.

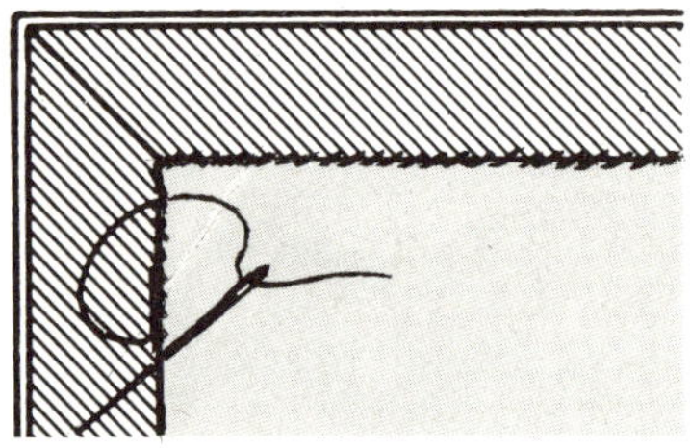

For the scalloped mat, fold the bias binding and tack in position. Fold to a mitre at the points. Back stitch or machine stitch.

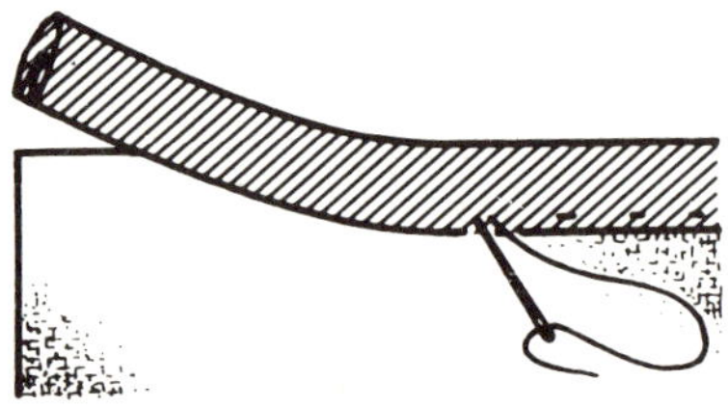

Canvas work stool

To assess the amount of canvas, measure vertically and horizontally across the centre of the stool, including the side drop. To each measurement allow at

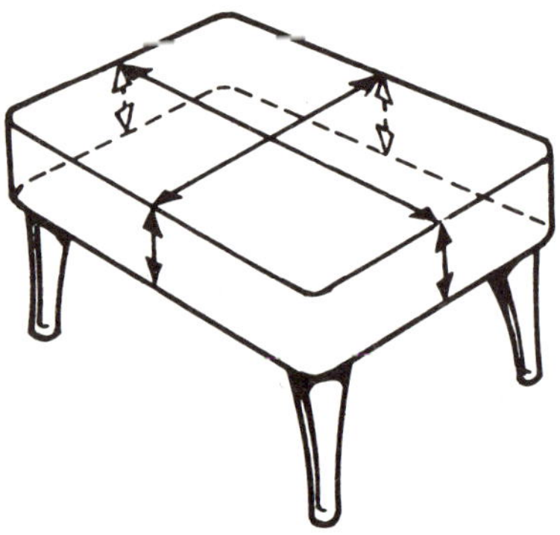

least 6 inches for stretching and making up. To mark the area of the canvas to be embroidered first measure the top of the stool. Outline this area with tacking stitches on the canvas, and extend the horizontal and vertical lines at each side for the depth of the side drop. Work the embroidery within these lines.

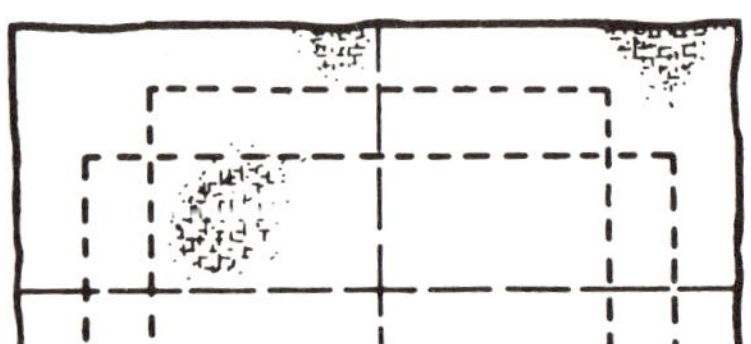

To cover the stool. Stretch the finished canvas, bring the right sides of the finished corners together as shown and back stitch close to the embroidery. Trim seam allowance at lower edge to 1½ inches. Turn the corner triangles to one side. Herringbone the corner and seam

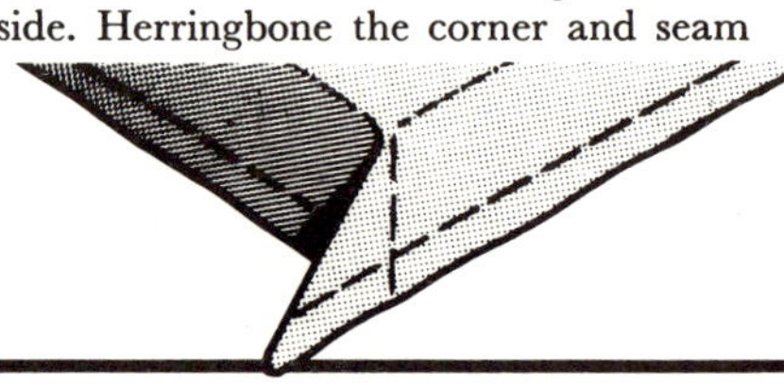

allowance in position at the back of the work. Turn to right side. Fit the cover to

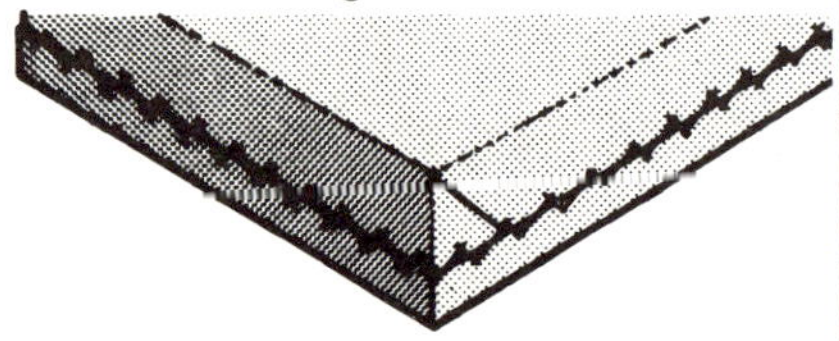

the stool. Working from the centres at each side, fix the canvas with brass headed tacks. Smooth the canvas into position as you work. Alternatively, plain tacks may be used and a decorative braid fixed at intervals to conceal them.

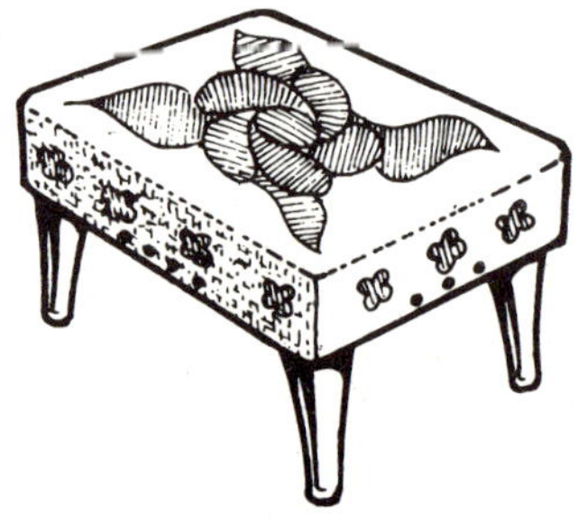

Making up cushions

Cushion pads and cushions are made to the same pattern to fit one within another. Make the cushion pad ½ inch smaller in each direction so that the cover will fit smoothly and slip on and off for washing. Fill the pad with foam rubber granules or kapok.

Circular cushion. Stitch round the seam line right sides together, leaving a gap to insert the filling. Cut out the

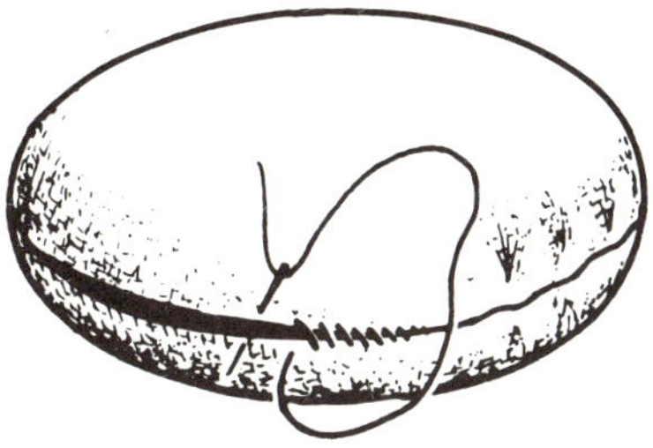

circle and clip at intervals for a smooth seam. Turn to right side, insert the pad and oversew the remaining few inches with small stitches in matching thread.

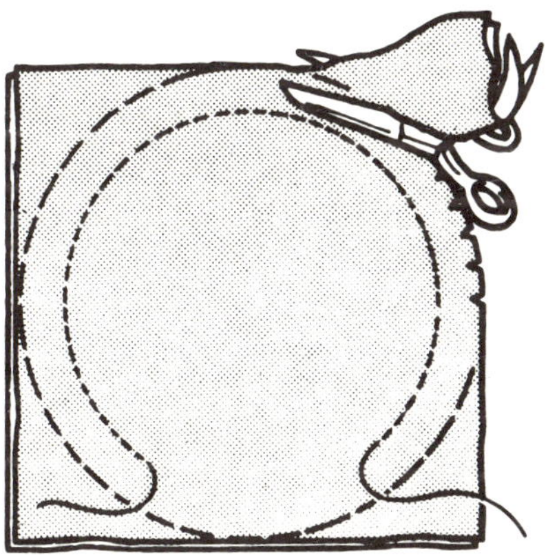

Square cushion. Make up in the same way. Clip corners and trim seam before turning to the right side.

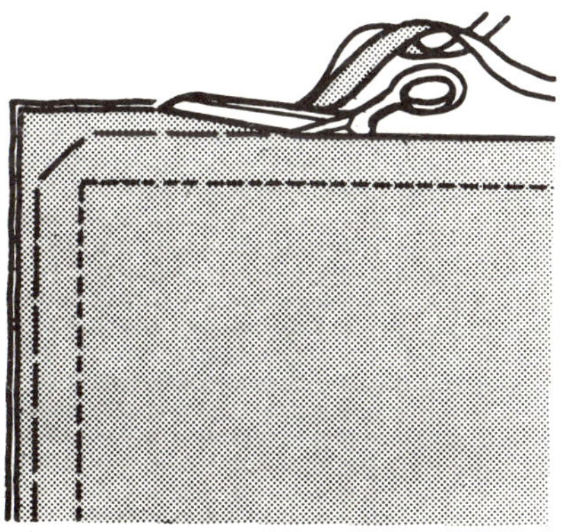

Cushion with gusset. Cut a strip of fabric of the required width and length, plus seam allowance. Stitch the two ends, right sides together. With right sides together, stitch the gusset to one side of the cushion. Repeat at the other side, leaving a gap to insert the pad.

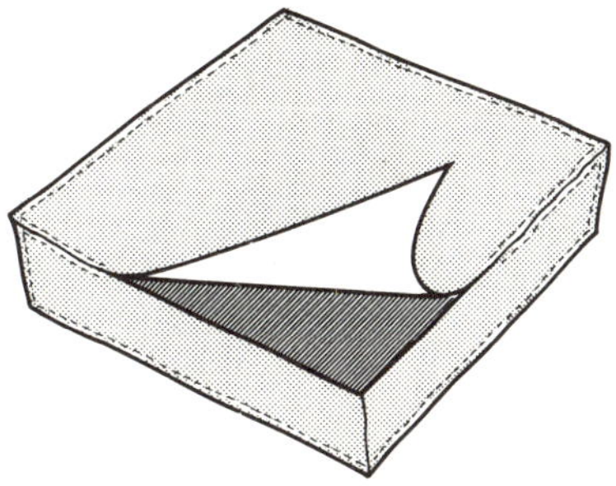

Trim seams and clip at corners. Turn to right side. Insert pad or filling and oversew as for the plain cushion.

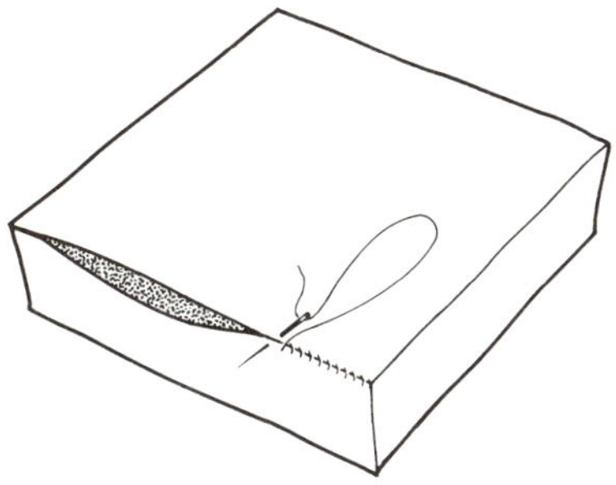

A piped edging for a cushion Measure the length of piping and bias binding required. Open out the binding and tack closely round the piping. Lay the two sides of the cushion right sides together and pin the piping between. The piping faces in to the centre of the cushion. Stitch three of the side seams. Leave the fourth seam open and stitch the piping to the front edge only. Turn to the right side, press lightly and insert the cushion pad. Fold the opening on the seam line and slip stitch to the back of the piping.

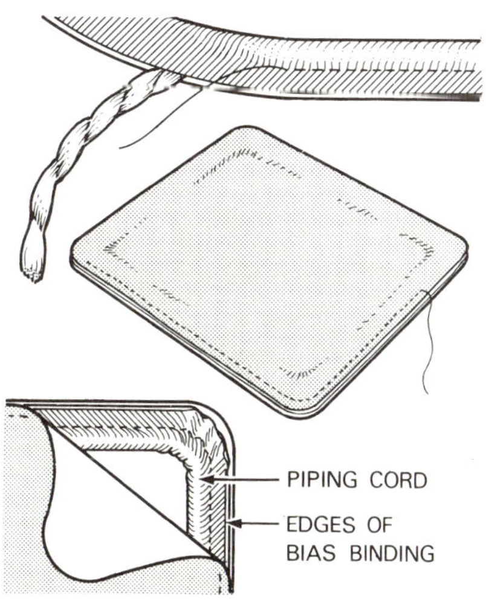

Making up a drop-in chair seat

Match the embroidery to the vertical and horizontal centres of the upholstery. Pin in place. Smooth and stretch evenly as you pin. Using chair tacks, (Diagram) fasten the canvas to the back of the seat. Check as you work to make sure that the embroidery is taut. Continue nailing, working outward from the centres. Fold the corners in neatly and tack closely for extra strength.

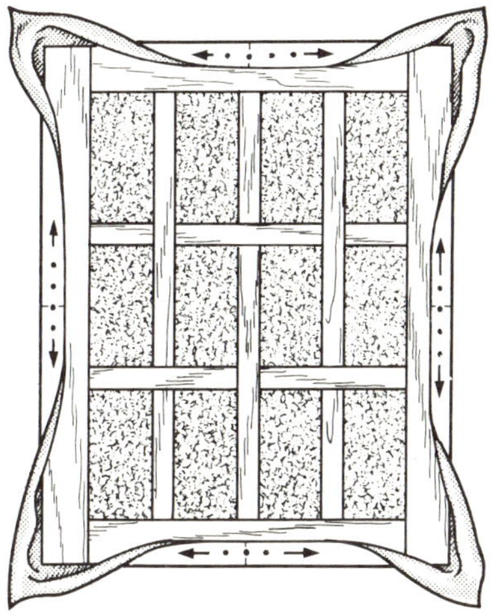

Jar tops

Cut the card circles and trim the canvas work to about half an inch. Mark the centres and match the card to the embroidery. Turn the seam allowance over the card, clipping the curves to make a smooth circle and fasten securely with fabric glue (Diagram). Allow to harden, then stick to the lid of the jar with a liberal amount of adhesive. Spot the edge of the lid with glue and stick the braid trim in position.

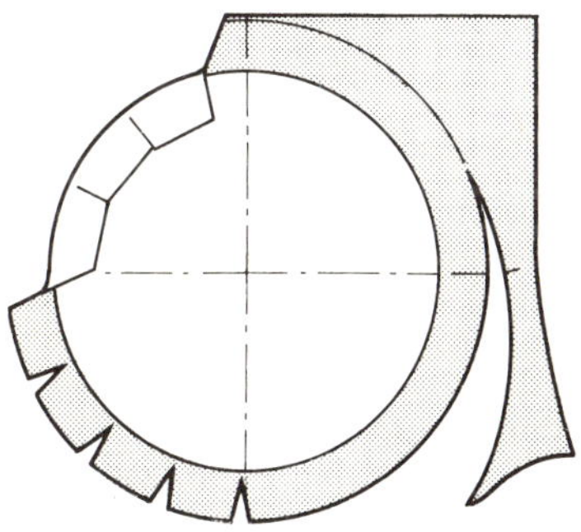

Making the mirror frame

From one of the pieces of cardboard, cut a rectangle for the frame as shown on the tracing pattern. Stretch the embroidery over the cardboard and secure the seam allowance at the back with fabric glue. Cut the center diagonally (Diagram 1) toward the corners. Turn in and stick a seam allowance to the back of the cardboard. Trim to half an inch. On the second piece of cardboard, glue the mirror in place to match the frame opening. Thread rings, for hanging, with tape and stick to the cardboard with fabric glue. (Diagram 2) Cover with a square of strong paper for extra security. When the glue has set, stick the two cardboard sections together.

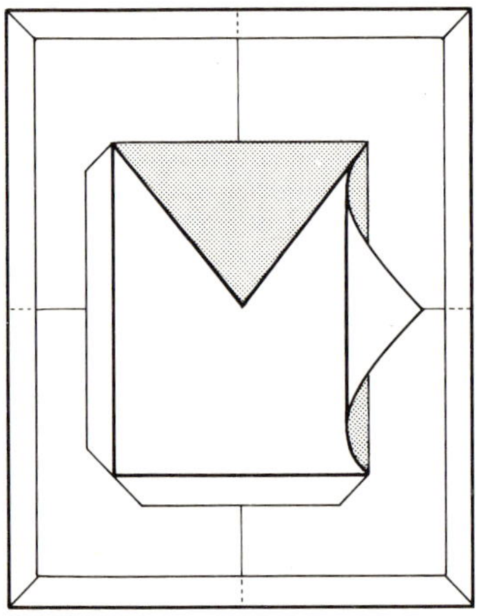

DIAGRAM 1

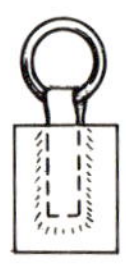

DIAGRAM 2

stitch library

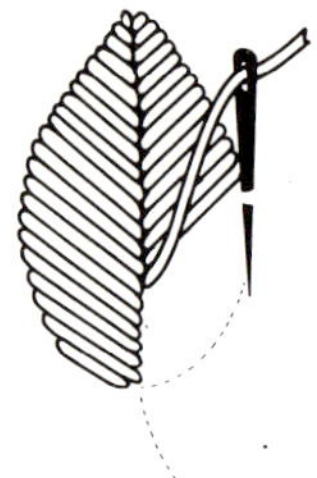

Surface satin stitch

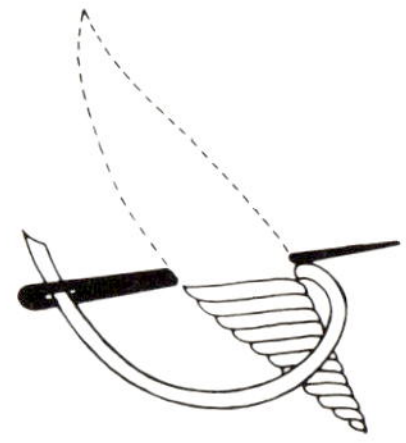

Satin stitch

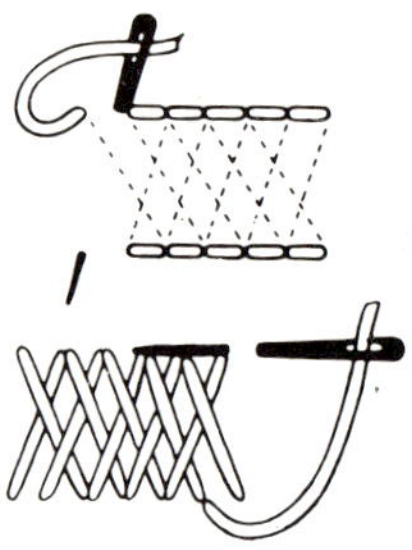

Herringbone stitch (open)

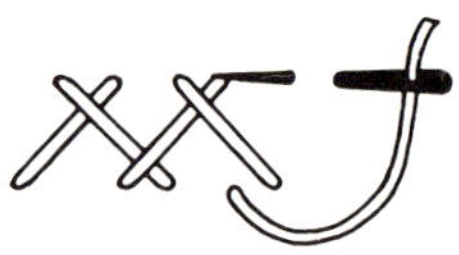

Herringbone stitch (closed)

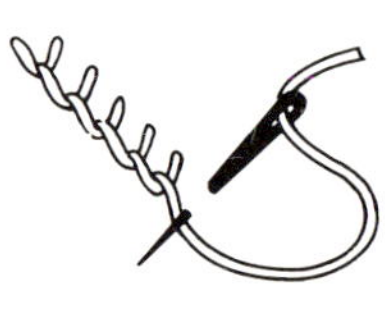

Feather stitch (half)

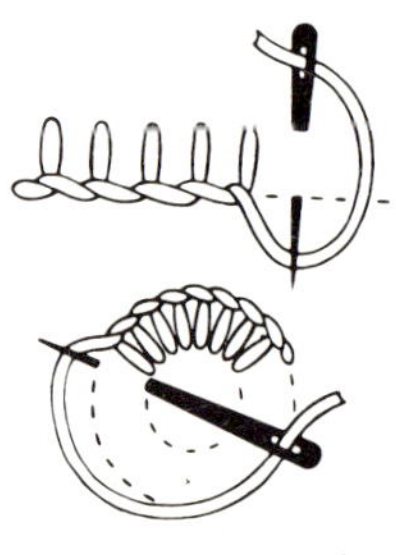

Blanket stitch

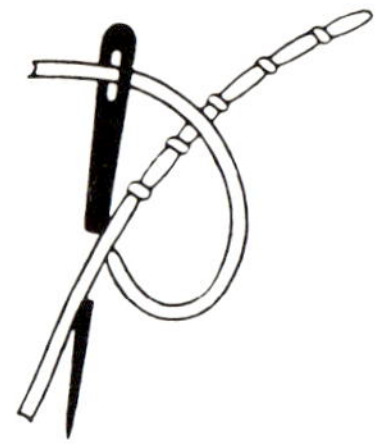

Couching

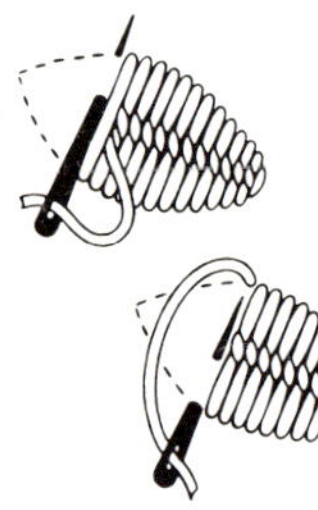

Rumanian stitch

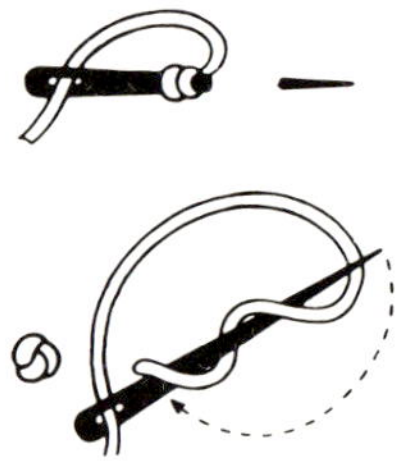

French knot

Chain stitch

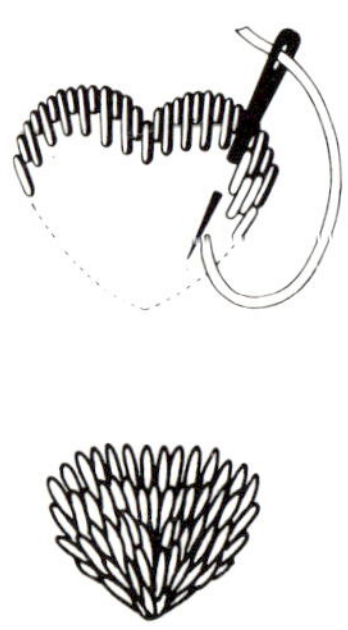

Long and short stitch

Running stitch

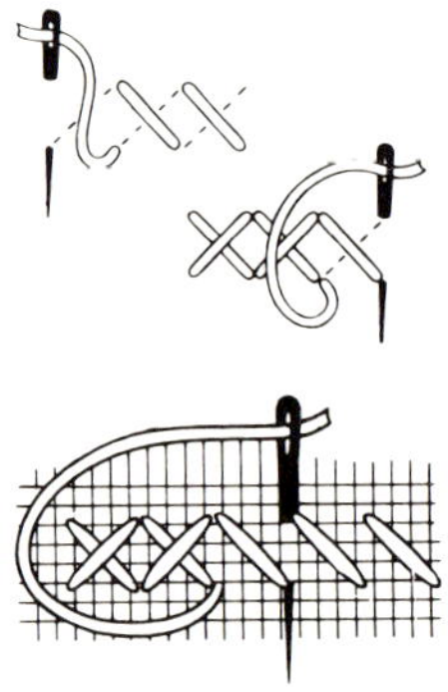

Cross stitch

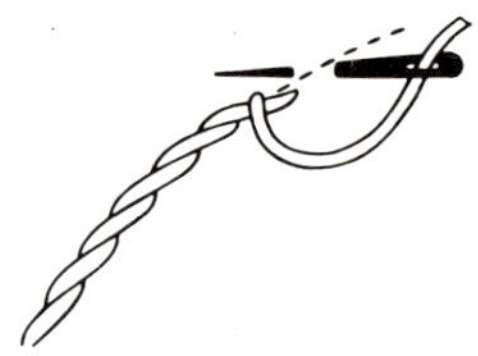

Outline stitch

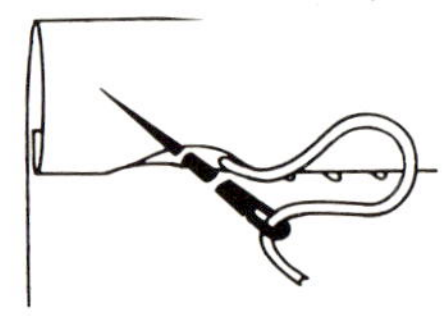

Slip stitch

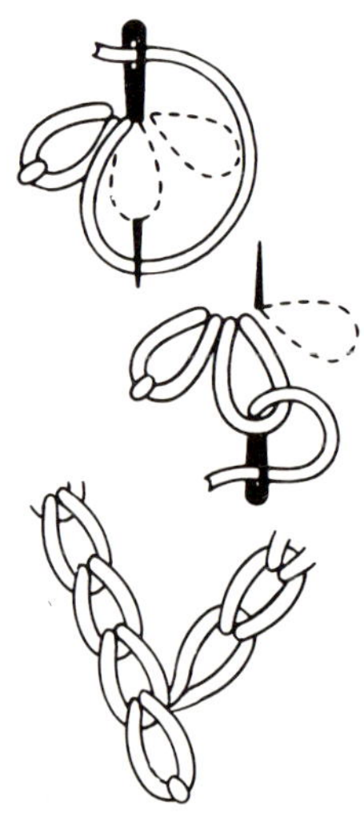

Detached chain